A Symposium on Creation

A Symposium on Creation

by

Henry M. Morris and Others

BAKER BOOK HOUSE
Grand Rapids, Michigan

Library of Congress Catalog Card Number: 68-19213

ISBN: 0-8010-5887-2

First printing, April 1968
Second printing, September 1969
Third printing, September 1971

PHOTOLITHOPRINTED BY CUSHING - MALLOY, INC.
ANN ARBOR, MICHIGAN, UNITED STATES OF AMERICA
1971

FOREWORD

Two of the most vigorous and promising developments in the field of learning in our day have sprung up independently over the past ten or twenty years. Now they are being joined together in what should be another great stride toward leadership in the modern realm of thought.

The first of these is the re-establishment of belief in the historic fact of creation as the fundamental postulate of natural science; the other is the re-establishment of schooling as a religious work and the reappearance of Christian schools in every part of the land.

The papers presented in this volume represent the bringing together of these two developments. They were delivered by men of science, leaders in what may be called creation research, at the annual conference on Christian schooling in Houston, Texas, under the auspices of the Association for Christian Schools.

This conference, held at St. Thomas' Episcopal School, is attended largely by teachers and administrators of Christian schools from all over the country, from many denominations. There are no member schools either of the conference or of the association: attendance is open to all who wish to come, and the whole purpose is to stimulate a recovery of the high standards of Christian learning — without question the most exacting known to man.

There is no attempt made to impose any of the thinking of the conference on those in attendance. The criterion for selection of speakers is that they be convinced of the truth of creation as it has been believed by Christians always, and that they explore the implications of this fact on their various disciplines.

It would be rash indeed to expect complete and settled doctrines at this stage, or perhaps ever, except in theology. Even here, where theological doctrines seem to be open to differences without departing from the doctrine of creation, no agreement is required. Clearly there must be a great deal of exploratory work done in the sciences, and there must be ample room for trial and error, for honest mistakes, for readjustment to new facts. Perhaps there is no limit to the facts that have to be interpreted or reinterpreted in the light of the controlling belief in creation.

The scholars engaged in this pursuit would probably be among the first to insist that their work is not definitive, and that at the present writing the most that can be hoped for is to lay the foundation for a whole new system of scientific thought. It must also be recognized that men of religion who have sought to reconcile evolutionary premises with Christian doctrine also have some hard thinking and study to do.

Undoubtedly one of the strongest forces directing the new line of interpretation has been that of so-called scientific investigation itself. It is men of science more than men of religion who are leading the return to the doctrine of Creation. New findings have amassed an overwhelming body of data that simply cannot be accommodated to the twin pillars of evolutionary thought — eons of time and chance. On the other hand, the doctrine of creation offers an exciting basis for interpretation and as more and more work is done along this line, the greater is the response from all sides.

One of the leaders in this field, Dr. A. E. Wilder Smith, professor of pharmacology at the University of Illinois Medical Center, Chicago, has written: "Darwin, when he formulated his theories of the origin of life one hundred years ago, had no knowledge of either the laws of thermodynamics (they were just being worked out by Calusius, Clapeyron, and Kelvin at that time), or the laws of heredity (Mendel's laws were unknown to him, though published in Darwin's lifetime). Darwin in his day could therefore assume with impunity that order did arise spontaneously from chaos, that life did arise spontaneously. Today, in the light of scientific discovery, we can no longer do this."

It is a rare privilege to be associated with men of such intellectual skill and courage and to be in any way connected with the great contribution they are making to the whole field of learning and especially to the recovery of Christian scholarship, the jewel of human achievement. Their papers are to be commended to all who are concerned with Truth.

T. Robert Ingram

TABLE OF CONTENTS

Science versus Scientism

by Henry M. Morris

DR. HENRY M. MORRIS

Dr. Morris has been Professor of Hydraulic Engineering and Chairman of the Department of Civil Engineering at the Virginia Polytechnic Institute; since 1957. His education includes a B.S. "with distinction" from Rice University, in 1939, and the M.S. and Ph.D. degrees from the University of Minnesota, in 1948 and 1950, respectively. He spent three years with the International Boundary and Water Commission, first as Junior Engineer, then as Assistant Hydraulic Engineer, followed by four years on the civil engineering faculty at Rice. He was on the faculty of the University of Minnesota during the period 1946-1951, and was Professor and Head of the Civil Engineering Department at Southwestern Louisiana University from 1951 through 1956. A full Member of Sigma Xi, an Honor Member of Chi Epsilon, and a Member of Phi Beta Kappa and Tau Beta Pi, all honorary societies, he is a Fellow of the American Society of Civil Engineers and of the American Association for Advancement of Science, and holds professional memberships in the American Geophysical Union, the American Meteorological Society, the International Commission for Irrigation and Drainage Research, and others. Dr. Morris is Chairman of the Applied Hydraulics Committee of the American Society for Engineering Education, is a member of various other regional and national committees, and has biographical listings in six different "Who's Who" publications.

I

SCIENCE VERSUS SCIENTISM
IN HISTORICAL GEOLOGY

The study of historical geology holds great fascination for many people who are neither historians nor geologists. This discipline occupies a uniquely interesting and important position in human thought. Among the humanities, the study of history surely is of singular significance and, among the sciences, geology, dealing as it does with the very earth itself, is similarly of unique interest. When the two are combined in historical geology, which professes to be able to decipher the mystery of the origin and history of the earth and its processes, the resulting panorama is of marvelous interest and significance. Such a picture, in fact, is of far more than historical and geological pertinence. Anything which elucidates origins is necessarily of philosophical and theological interest, with strong implications regarding meanings and purposes and destinies as well.

It is little wonder, then, that historical geology has attracted the intense interest and concern of a great variety of people. As a matter of fact, the basic structure of modern historical geology was worked out over a hundred years ago by such men as James Hutton (an agriculturalist with medical training), John Playfair (a mathematician), William Smith (a surveyor), Charles Lyell (a lawyer), Georges Cuvier (a comparative anatomist), Charles Darwin (an apostate divinity student and naturalist), Robert Chambers (a journalist), William Buckland (a theologian), Roderick Murchison (a soldier and gentleman of leisure), Adam Sedgwick (who, when seeking election to the chair of geology at Cambridge, boasted that he knew nothing of geology), Hugh Miller (a stonemason), John Fleming (a zoologist), and others of like assortment.

Although the basic framework of historical geology, as worked out by these men, has not changed to the present day, there has arisen a group of specialists in historical geology who have come to regard this field as their own particular field of *science*, and who now regard with some disdain any who venture to write or speak in this field without giving full allegiance to the accepted system. By its very nature, however, historical geology is not, and can never be, a genuine *science*, and therefore the dogmatic

11

insistence that one follow the interpretations of its founders and present-day leaders, with all the implications of origins and meanings that are involved, is nothing less than *scientism*.

This is in no way meant to be a reflection upon the science of geology, which is a true science in every sense of the word, and which has made a tremendous contribution to our understanding and application of the laws of nature. When, however, a geologist (or lawyer or surveyor or naturalist or anything else) seeks to become a *historical* geologist, he must leave the realm of science and enter that of philosophy or religion. The presently accepted system of historical geology is basically nothing else than a philosophy or a religion of evolutionary uniformitarianism. If this fact were only recognized and acknowledged by its adherents, no one would be greatly disturbed, but when this system is widely promulgated and insisted upon in the name of *science*, it has degenerated into mere scientism instead. This will become more evident as we consider the true meaning of science and the true nature of those physical processes studied by science.

What Is Science?

The word "science" itself, of course, is derived from the Latin *scientia* ("knowledge"), and this is essentially what it means. A more formal definition, as given in the Oxford dictionary, is as follows: "A branch of study which is concerned either with a connected body of demonstrated truths or with observed facts systematically classified and more or less colligated by being brought under general laws, and which includes trustworthy methods for the discovery of new truth within its own domain."

Science thus involves facts which are observed and laws which have been demonstrated. The scientific method involves experimental reproducibility, with like causes producing like effects. It is *knowledge*, not inference or speculation or extrapolation.

True science thus is necessarily limited to the measurement and study of *present* phenomena and processes. Data which have been actually observed in the present, or which have been recorded by human observers in the historic past, are properly called scientific data. Laws which have been deduced from these data, which satisfactorily correlate the pertinent data and which have predictive value for the correlation of similar data obtained from like experiments in the future, are properly regarded as scientific laws.

But there is obviously no way of knowing that these processes and the laws which describe them have always been the same in the past or that they will always be the same in the future. It is possible to make an assumption of this kind, of course, and this is the well-known principle of *uniformitarianism*. The assumption is reasonable, in the light of our experience with present processes, and it is no doubt safe to extrapolate on this basis for a certain time into the future and back into the past. But to insist that uniformitarianism is the only scientific approach to the understanding of *all* past and future time is clearly nothing but a dogmatic tenet of a particular form of religion.

That uniformitarianism has been the foundational and guiding principle of historical geology is widely recognized. A standard textbook on the subject says, for example:

> The uprooting of such fantastic beliefs (that is, those of the catastrophists—author) began with the Scottish geologist, James Hutton, whose *Theory of the Earth*, published in 1785, maintained that the *present is the key to the past* and that, given sufficient time, processes now at work could account for all the geologic features of the Globe. This philosophy, which came to be known as the *doctrine of uniformitarianism* demands an immensity of time; it has now gained universal acceptance among intelligent and informed people.[1]

Thus, science deals with the data and processes of the present, which can be experimentally measured and observationally verified. The principle of uniformity is a philosophy, or faith, by which it is hoped that these processes of the present can be extrapolated into the distant past and the distant future to explain all that has ever happened and to predict all that will ever happen.

But, when viewed in these terms, it is obvious that uniformity is not proved, and therefore is not properly included in the definition of science. There may be any number of other assumptions which might serve as the basis of such extrapolation, and all would similarly be mere acts of faith.

It is perfectly possible and reasonable, as we shall see, to assume that the processes studied by science were themselves created at some time in the past and will be terminated at some time in the future. The processes themselves then could tell us nothing about their creation or termination — this would be outside the domain of scientific investigation. Such information could come, if at all, only by revelation from their Creator.

---

[1]Carl O. Dunbar, *"Historical Geology"* (2nd. Ed., New York: John Wiley and Sons, 1960), p. 18. Emphasis is his.

As a matter of fact, a full and complete understanding of any process, even in its present character, could in that case be obtained only in the context and framework of the fact of its prior creation. This is because *meaning* is inextricably inter-related with *origin* and *destiny*.

Apart from this structure, however, it is possible and proper to study science, in the sense of present processes, without reference to the past or future. Thus, the science of physics deals with the present processes of the physical world; the science of chemistry deals with the present chemical properties and behavior of matter; the science of geology deals with present geological processes and earth features; the science of biology deals with the processes of life in plants, animals and man. So long as the question of *origins* or *ends* is not considered, there will be no conflict between the Bible and science. The Bible has numerous references to present phenomena of science, and all will be found in strict accord with the actual observed data. It is only when questions of origins or destinies (or fundamental meanings) are considered that conflicts appear.

To a considerable degree, therefore, a *Christian* study of physics or chemistry or other science can proceed along the same lines as a treatment by non-Christians. The same textbooks can be used, the same experimental apparatus, the same methods, provided only that the study is limited to an elucidation of the actual present properties and processes of the data of that science. But as soon as intrinsic meanings or origins or destinies are brought into the treatment, there will inevitably be conflict between the uniformitarian and Christian world-views.

The Processes of Science

Assuming that our study of science will be, as is proper, limited to the study of present processes, we soon encounter a most remarkable and significant fact. Regardless of the particular discipline of science we study — physics, chemistry, biology, geology, etc. — these processes all are built upon two basic concepts and follow two basic laws. The two basic concepts are *energy* and *entropy*, and the two laws are the *first and second laws of thermodynamics*.

Since the implications of these laws are highly important to the Christian cosmology, it will be well to allow a non-theist, thoroughly evolutionary and uniformitarian in his philosophy, to define them. Dr. Harold F. Blum, the Princeton biologist, states them as follows:

Energy appears in various forms: heat, kinetic energy, mechanical work, chemical energy, and so forth. Energy can change its form but not its quantity — this is a statement of the *first law of thermodynamics*, which until quite recently could be accepted without qualification. We know, now, that matter is another form of energy, but that does not alter this fundamental principle which is also called the law of conservation of energy.[2]

Energy is the concept which measures the capacity of doing work. Thus, everything in the physical universe, including matter and all the phenomena associated with matter, is essentially one or another form of energy. This first law of thermodynamics, which was proved empirically about a century ago, is really the most basic of all scientific laws. It has been verified in countless thousands of experiments, ranging from those on the scale of the sub-nuclear particles to measurements of the stars and galaxies, and there is no known exception. Thus, according to this most basic and best-proved of all scientific laws, there is *nothing which is now being created or destroyed*. Present processes, with which alone true science is able to deal, are *not* processes of creation.

With respect to the second law, Blum continues:

> The *second law of thermodynamics* cannot be put in such concise form as the first; it is stated in numerous ways, according to the kind of problem under study. . . . It is one of this law's consequences that all real processes go irreversibly. Let us consider a universe in which the total amount of energy remains, supposedly, constant. Any given process in this universe is accompanied by a change in magnitude of a quantity called the *entropy*, . . . All real processes go with an increase of entropy. The entropy also measures the randomness or lack of orderliness of the system, the greater the randomness the greater the entropy; . . .[3]

Thus, the second law of thermodynamics states that there is a universal tendency toward disorder and decay. In any finite open system, of course, there may be temporarily and locally an increase of order, due to the influx of ordering energy from outside the system, but the tendency is always ultimately downward toward disintegration and death. This law also is proved beyond question, with no known exceptions. As Blum says, in the preface to the third edition of his book:

---

[2]*Time's Arrow and Evolution* (Torchbook Edition, New York: Harper and Brothers, 1962), p. 14.
[3]*Ibid*, pp. 14, 15.

> Wishful thinking to the contrary, the second law of thermo-
> dynamics remains with us; . . . no wise scientist will, I think, deny
> its existence or import.[4]

Since we are here specially concerned with geological processes,
the testimony of a prominent geologist will also be cited. Dr.
Brian Mason, who is Curator of Physical Geology and Mineralogy
at the American Museum of Natural History, says:

> In redistribution and recombination of the chemical elements in
> minerals and rocks the atoms or ions lose part of their energy and
> yield more stable systems. Every rock exemplifies the laws condi-
> tioning the stability of crystal lattices, laws which follow the gen-
> eral principles of the structure of matter and of thermodynamics
> . . . the study of equilibria in laboratory experiments and by
> thermodynamic methods has thrown a flood of light on geochemical
> reactions, such as the origin of rocks and minerals, the processes
> of weathering and decomposition, and other kinds of transforma-
> tions going on within the earth. . . . The major value of thermo-
> dynamics in geochemistry is that it provides a general approach to
> problems of stability, equilibrium, and chemical change.[5]

Thus, the two laws of thermodynamics are not simply laws of
physics and engineering, as they are too often considered to be,
but are universal laws governing the behavior of all matter and
processes on the earth, including those of biology, as Blum has
shown, and of geology, as Mason has shown. The first law teaches
that energy (which includes everything in the physical universe)
is quantitatively constant. The second law teaches that energy
is qualitatively deteriorating. Thus *the present processes of nature are not processes of creation and integration, but rather of
conservation and disintegration.*

All real processes in the universe, of course, therefore involve
change, which means essentially exchanges of energy, or trans-
formations of energy from one kind into another. But these
changes are basically processes of decay. Locally and temporarily
there may be processes which seem to be processes of growth
and integration (such as the growth of a child or the growth of
a crystal or the manufacture of an automobile). But these are
due to a temporary excess influx of ordering energy into the
system. Eventually, though, the child will grow old and die, the
crystal will disintegrate, and the automobile will end up in the

---

[4]*Ibid*, p. v.
[5]*Principles of Geochemistry* (2nd. Ed., New York: John Wiley & Sons,
   Inc., 1960), pp. 64, 68.

auto graveyard. Most processes fail even to exhibit this tentative growth character. In geology, for example, the typical processes are those of erosion, heat flow, radioactive decay, etc. In fact, it is such processes as these whose measured rates have served as the basis for geochronological calculations. But here a very important caution is in order. Although the second law of thermodynamics indicates that any system must decay, it says nothing about the rate of decay. As Mason says:

> It is important to realize, however, that thermodynamics cannot predict the *rate* at which a reaction will proceed and does not tell us anything of the mechanism of the reaction.[6]

And, similarly, Blum says:

> The second law of thermodynamics points the direction of events in time, but does not tell when or how fast they will go.[7]

These rates of decay will depend upon many variables, and in nearly all cases must be determined empirically, by actual measurements. There is never any assurance that the decay rates will be constant, as they may well change if the factors which influence them change. All geochronometers are suspect from this cause alone.

The True Uniformitarianism

We now can see that the concept of uniformitarianism, while perfectly valid and proper in its legitimate framework, has been applied quite illegitimately in historical geology. True uniformity has to do with the inviolability of natural *law* (e.g., the laws of thermodynamics), and not with the uniformity of process *rates*. The laws of thermodynamics indicate what the character of all natural processes must be, but they do not indicate how fast or how slow such processes will proceed. And there certainly is never any assurance that the rate of any given process will always be constant.

But it is this assumed uniformity of process rates which is at the very hub of the principle of uniformity as it has been applied in historical geology. This is evident from the following rather typical descripton of the principle:

> Opposed to this line of thinking was Sir Charles Lyell (1797-1875), a contemporary of Cuvier, who held that earth changes were

---

[6]*Ibid*, p. 68.
[7]*Op. cit.*, p. 16.

gradual, taking place at the same uniform slowness that they are today. Lyell is thus credited with the propagation of the premise that more or less has guided geological thought ever since, namely, that *the present is the key to the past*. In essence, Lyell's *doctrine of uniformitarianism* stated that past geological processes operated in the same manner and at the same rate they do today.[8]

Now it is quite obvious that if geological processes have always been going on at the same slow rates they exhibit today, the earth must be immensely old. Age calculations by certain of these processes — such as radioactive decay, continental erosion, canyon-cutting, deltaic deposition, oceanic sodium increments, etc. — when based on present rates, are, of course, bound to give extremely high values, far greater than can possibly be accommodated within the framework of Biblical chronology.

But there is clearly no scientific basis for assuming such uniformity of process rates. It is quite valid to assume that running water will erode soil and rock, that radioactive minerals will decay, and that all other such processes will proceed irreversibly, in accord with the second law of thermodynamics, but neither this nor any other scientific law provides any guarantee that such rates will always be slow and uniform. In fact, it is certain that all such real decay processes are so intricately complex and are affected by such a great number of factors (a change in any one of which may drastically affect the process rate) that it will forever be quite impossible to say exactly what the rate will be except under very precisely known and experimentally confirmed conditions.

It is encouraging that many geologists in recent years are beginning to recognize and acknowledge this distinction. For example, Zumberge, in a widely used introductory text, after defining uniformitarianism as above, cautions:

> From a purely scientific point of view, it is unwise to accept uniformitarianism as unalterable dogma. As pointed out in chapter one, man's experience with geological processes is restricted to only a minute fraction of the total span of earth history. He should never close his mind to the possibility that conditions in past geological time were different than today, and that the doctrine of uniformitarianism may not apply in every case where the reconstruction of some segment of earth history is involved.[9]

---

[8]James H. Zumberge, *Elements of Geology* (2nd. Ed., New York: John Wiley and Sons, Inc., 1963), p. 200. Emphasis is his.

[9]*Ibid*, p. 201.

A very strong statement of the pitfalls of uniformitarianism in attempting to explain the sedimentary rocks is given by a member of the geology faculty at Pennsylvania State University:

> Conventional uniformitarianism, or "gradualism," i.e., the doctrine of unchanging change, is verily contradicted by all post-Cambrian sedimentary data and the geotectonic histories of which these sediments are the record. Thus, quantitative interpretations of the Ordovician from the Recent are meaningless.[10]

More recently, a Columbia University geologist has clearly tried to distinguish between the true and the fallacious uniformitarianism (calling them methodological and substantive uniformitarianism, respectively):

> Uniformitarianism is a dual concept. Substantive uniformitarianism (a testable theory of geologic change postulating uniformity of rates or material conditions) is false and stifling to hypothesis formation. Methodological uniformitarianism (a procedural principle asserting spatial and temporal invariance of natural laws) belongs to the definition of science and is not unique to geology.[11]

With this we would heartily agree. Uniformity of natural laws is basic in science, and is quite in accord with Scripture (always allowing, of course, for the possible miraculous interruption of those laws by the Creator when He so wills). But the type of geological uniformitarianism which has held sway for a hundred years, and which has indeed served as the very foundation of the theory of evolution, is not only contrary to the Biblical record, but is completely inadequate to explain the actual data of geology.

> Substantive uniformitarianism as a descriptive theory has not withstood the test of new data and can no longer be maintained in any strict manner.[12]

Since geological uniformitarianism in the traditional sense can no longer be maintained, and since uniformitarianism in the true sense is in no way a peculiar possession of the science of geology, it is thus completely wrong to refer to uniformitarianism as being in some way particularly the possession of geological theory. An

[10]P. D. Krynine, "Uniformitarianism Is a Dangerous Doctrine," *Journal of Paleontology*, Volume 30, 1956, p. 1004.
[11]Stephen Jay Gould, "Is Uniformitarianism Necessary?" *American Journal of Science*, Volume 263, March 1965, p. 223.
[12]*Ibid*, p. 226.

illuminating admission giving the reason why this identification
continues to be made is revealed in the following:

> As a special term, methodological uniformitarianism was useful
> only when science was debating the status of the supernatural in
> its realm; for if God intervenes, then laws are not invariant and
> induction becomes invalid. . . . The term today is an anachronism
> for we need no longer take special pains to affirm the scientific
> nature of our discipline.[13]

If one looks beneath the surface of these reasonings, he begins
to see that the real problem is not one of science at all, but of
scientism! That is, historical geologists have attempted to defend
substantive uniformitarianism (i.e., uniformity of process rates) by
citing the undisputed evidences of methodological uniformitarianism (i.e., uniformity of natural law). Whether this fallacy in
reasoning has been conscious or sub-conscious is really imma-
terial; the basic reason for it in either case, has been the innate
desire to relegate the position of the Creator and His possible
intervention in history as far back in time as possible, and perhaps even to eliminate Him altogether. A full-orbed philosophy
— nay, a religion, — of origins and development has thus been
erected upon a fallacious uniformitarianism. And this is scientism,
not science.

The Evolutionary Framework

The vast ages of earth history which supposedly are implied
by the principle of uniformity have been subdivided into a more
or less standard series of geological eras and periods, each with
a generally accepted name and approximate duration. The whole
sequence is known as the Geological Column, and the corresponding chronology is known as the Geological Time Scale. This,
of course, is the very backbone of the so-called historical geology.
Any given rock formation must occupy a certain position in the
Column, and presumably it can be dated as to time of formation
in terms of the Time Scale.

A highly pertinent question needs asking at this point. On
what basis are the various rock types and formations identified
and classified? How is one system assigned to, say, the Devonian
Period and another to the Ordovician? How do we know which
is older and which is younger? How are the divisions between
successive periods recognized?

---

[13]*Ibid*, p. 227.

As a matter of fact, this problem of stratigraphic classification is involved in no little uncertainty and controversy at the present time, even though the Geologic Time Scale has been generally accepted in its present form for about a hundred years.

The layman is inclined to assume that the principle of superposition is the main factor in determining relative age, and that equivalent strata in different areas can be recognized by their chemical or physical composition. However, this is not so. The factor which is by all odds the most important in assigning an age to a given stratum is its biological content — that is, the *fossils* it contains.

> Thus it appears that the only presently available rational geochronological indices are biostratigraphically based — i.e., *biochronologic.*[14]

This means plainly that *only* the fossils can be relied upon as a criterion for determining the time in earth history when a particular formation was deposited. Other data — vertical position, physico-chemical characteristics, and other factors — are essentially insignificant.

> Physico-geometrical data (apart from radiometric) can do no more than provide a crude local relative chronology or circumstantial evidence in support of a biochronologic framework.[15]

Now the only way in which the fossil contents of a rock could possibly indicate how old the rock might be is if the animals found as fossils were living only at that specific time in earth history. This means that there have been different kinds of life at different periods in history, and that therefore the living forms provide an unambiguous index to the chronology.

But how do we know which forms were living then? There must be some systematic way of viewing and classifying the changes of life forms with the passage of geologic time. The key, of course, is evolution! If we are to explain everything in terms of uniform laws and uniform processes, this must include the development of the biological world as well as the physical world. All kinds of animals therefore must have gradually developed from earlier and simpler forms. There must have been a slow increase of organization and complexity of living forms dur-

---

[14]T. G. Miller, "Time in Stratigraphy," *Paleontology*, Volume 8, February, 1965, p. 119. Emphasis his. Miller is at Keele University in Staffordshire.
[15]*Ibid*, p. 128.

ing geologic history. And this is the clue we need! Simple fossils mean a formation is ancient; complex fossils are recent.

The fossil record thus is of absolutely paramount importance in geologic dating. The fossil forms are classified according to the underlying evolutionary assumptions, and then they in turn become "index fossils" for future dating purposes.

> In each sedimentary stratum certain fossils seem to be characteristically abundant: these fossils are known as *index fossils*. If in a strange formation an index fossil is found, it is easy to date that particular layer of rock and to correlate it with other exposures in distant regions containing the same species.[16]

The evolutionary significance of this methodology is clearly indicated by the following:

> Once it was understood that each fossil represents a biologic entity, instead of a special divinely created life form, it became quite obvious that the plants and animals of each stratigraphic division had simply evolved from those of the preceding epoch through gradual adaptation. They were, in turn, ancestral to those that followed.[17]

This technique might have merit if it were actually known, from historical records or from divine revelation or from some other source, that in fact all living forms had actually evolved from prior forms. But the actual evidence for evolution on such a scale as this is, as implied by the above quotation, limited to the fossil record itself. In a presidential address before the Geological Society of America, Hollis H. Hedberg also stressed the evolutionary significance of the fossil record, as follows:

> That our present-day knowledge of the sequence of strata in the earth's crust is in major part due to the evidence supplied by fossils is a truism. Merely in their role as distinctive rock constituents, fossils have furnished one of the best and most widely used means of tracing beds and correlating them. However, going far beyond this fossils have furnished, through their record of the evolution of life on this planet, an amazingly effective key to the relative positioning of strata in widely separated regions and from continent to continent.[18]

---

[16]J. E. Ransom, *Fossils in America* (New York: Harper & Row, 1964), p. 43.

[17]*Ibid.*

[18]"The Stratigraphic Panorama," *Geological Society of America Bulletin*, Volume 72, April 1961, pp. 499-518.

Thus, the primary means of dating rock formations relative to each other, in the Geologic Column, is the evolutionary sequence of life on the earth through geologic time, and the preservation of distinctive life forms as fossils deposited in the rocks laid down during each successive period. But, then, in turn, the history of evolution on the earth has been built up on the basis of the record revealed in the rocks representing the successive geological ages. In fact, the only genuine historical evidence for the truth of evolution is found in this fossil record. As Dunbar says:

> Although the comparative study of living plants and animals may give very convincing circumstantial evidence, fossils provide the only historical, documentary evidence that life has evolved from simpler to more and more complex forms.[19]

The evidence for evolution afforded by living plants and animals is, indeed, hardly convincing at all. The almost universally accepted biologic mechanism for producing evolutionary change is supposed to be genetic mutation (a sudden, random change in the biochemical structure of the germ cell) preserved, if favorable, by natural selection.

This is confirmed by the very prominent Edinburgh geneticist, C. H. Waddington:

> It remains true to say that we know of no way other than random mutation by which new hereditary variation comes into being, nor any process other than natural selection by which the hereditary constitution of a population changes from one generation to the next.[20]

Since our focus of attention in this chapter is geology, we do not wish to digress into a discussion of genetic theory at this point, except to call attention to the fact that *present* processes of biologic change are associated almost exclusively with mutations as far as permanent, hereditary, truly novel changes are concerned. Presumably if evolution is actually a fact of nature, it is to be explained in terms of mutation and natural selection. This, in fact, is undoubtedly the consensus of the thinking of most leading evolutionists today, not only those working in the field of genetics, but also those in the field of paleontology.

Furthermore, it is admitted by all geneticists that the great majority — in fact, almost *all* — mutations are basically harmful.

---

[19]*Op. cit,* p. 47.
[20]*The Nature of Life* (New York: Atheneum, 1961), p. 98.

This is only to be expected, since they represent random changes in very highly-ordered systems:

> Mutations occur at random, not because it would be convenient to have one. Any chance alteration in the composition and properties of a highly complex operating system is not likely to improve its manner of operation and most mutations are disadvantageous for this reason. There is a delicate balance between an organism and its environment which a mutation can easily upset. One could as well expect that altering the position of the foot brake or the gas pedal at random would improve the operation of an automobile.[21]

As a matter of fact, mutations provide a very fine illustration of the second law of thermodynamics — the universal tendency toward disorder and decay. In any case, truly beneficial mutations are obviously such very rare events, if they occur at all, that it is quite impossible to see real evolution occurring among present plants and animals. There is, of course, a great deal of variation, within basic kinds of creatures — in fact, no two individuals are exactly alike — but there are also quite clear-cut gaps between such basic kinds of creatures.

Since evolution cannot be demonstrated as occurring in the present, and since, indeed, such evidence as does exist of biologic change in the present seems to be evidence of decay and death, rather than growth and increasing organization, it is obvious that, in the last analysis, the only real evidence for evolution in the broad sense is that contained in the fossil record.

But the fossil record is based on the geologic ages, and the geologic ages have been built up as an interpretive framework for earth history on the very basis of the assumption of evolution! This is obviously circular reasoning, but that in itself does not condemn it since, in the final analysis, all philosophies are based on circular reasoning. One always brings certain innate presuppositions with him when he tries to philosophize on origins and meanings, and these necessarily determine his conclusions. It is only when such circular reasoning is called *science* that it really becomes scientism. As a religious faith, it may be a live option, but not as science!

Basic Inconsistencies in Evolutionary Uniformitarianism

The fallacious application of uniformitarian reasoning to geological process rates thus has led to the system of the evolutionary

---

[21]Frederick S. Hulse, *The Human Species* (New York: Random House, 1963), p. 53.

geologic ages. This in turn forms the evidential basis of the theory of evolution, which presumably accounts for the origin and development of all things, including life and including man. All of this, as we have just seen, involves a powerful system of circular reasoning, somewhat disguised but nonetheless real.

But there is another, perhaps even more significant, fallacy in this system, which will now be discussed. True uniformitarianism involves the constancy and reliability of natural laws. These laws are formulated to describe the processes of nature, and by their very nature, as concepts developed by scientific measurements and methods, these processes are known only in their *present* form. As noted earlier, these laws deal basically with the concepts of energy and entropy, and are ultimately structured around the two laws of thermodynamics.

The most basic and universal of all scientific laws is that of conservation. There are, of course, a number of different conservation laws (energy, mass, momentum, electric charge, etc), but the most important is that of energy (including mass, as a form of energy).

> The physicist's confidence in the conservation principles rests on long and thoroughgoing experience. The conservation of energy, of momentum and of electric charge have been found to hold, within the limits of accuracy of measurement, in every case that has been studied. An elaborate structure of physical theory has been built on these fundamental concepts, and its predictions have been confirmed without fail.[22]

Thus, the basic structure of the universe, in so far as *science* knows it, is conservative. That is, nothing is now being created or destroyed. The present processes of nature, including all geologic processes and all biologic processes, are not creative in nature.

Consequently, it is fundamentally impossible for science to learn anything about origins. Science deals with present processes, and present processes are conservative, not creative. Thus, historical geology, professing to discover the history of the origin and evolution of the earth and its inhabitants through a scientific study and extrapolation of present processes, is a self-contradiction.

And the situation becomes even more contradictory when the second law of thermodynamics is considered. Not only is the universe basically conservative in quantity, but it is also basically degradational in quality.

---

[22]Gerald Feinberg and Maurice Goldhaber, "The Conservation Laws of Physics," *Scientific America*, Volume 209, October 1963, p. 36.

> Man has long been aware that his world has a tendency to fall
> apart. Tools wear out, fishing nets need repair, roofs leak, iron
> rusts, wood decays, loved ones sicken and die, relatives quarrel, and
> nations make war. . . . We instinctively resent the decay of orderly
> systems such as the living organism and work to restore such sys-
> tems to their former or even higher level of organization.[23]

Thus, all systems, no matter how large or how small, living or
non-living, tend to become disordered and disorganized, to decay
and die. Application of an excess of ordering energy from outside
the system is continually needed to offset this decadent tendency,
and even more is needed if, for a while, the system is to manifest
a period of growth and integration.

There could hardly be imagined a philosophy more in fundamental contradiction with this actual and unquestioned law of
nature than the philosophy of evolution. According to evolution,
there is an innate principle of development and progress in the
universe, leading always to higher and higher levels of complexity
and integration.

> Most enlightened persons now accept as a fact that everything in
> the cosmos — from heavenly bodies to human beings — has de-
> veloped and continues to develop through evolutionary processes.
> The great religions of the West have come to accept a historical
> view of creation. Evolutionary concepts are applied also to social
> institutions and to the arts. Indeed, most political parties, as well
> as schools of theology, sociology, history, or arts, teach these con-
> cepts and make them the basis of their doctrines. Thus, theoretical
> biology now pervades all of Western culture indirectly through
> the concept of progressive historical change.[24]

We would agree completely that modern science reveals a
concept of universal change — but this change is one of decay
and dissipation. The supposed universal process of evolution, on
the other hand, postulates a universal law of progress and increased organization. Thus, the theory of evolution and the second
law of thermodynamics squarely confront and contradict each
other. Each is precisely the converse of the other. One is a
universal law of change upward, the other a universal law of

---

[23]Van Rensselaer Potter, "Society and Science," *Science*, Volume 146,
   November 20, 1964, p. 1018.
[24]Rene Dubos, "Humanistic Biology," *American Scientest*, Volume 53,
   March 1965, p. 6.

change downward! It should be plain and obvious that only one of these principles can possibly be valid.

Herein is another, and climactic, contradiction in evolutionary historical geology. Historical geology purports to tell us of the evolutionary development of life on the earth, and to do so in terms of *present* processes. But present processes are processes of decay, and therefore contradict the very concept of evolution.

If historical geology would be truly scientific, as it claims to be, then it must recognize that it must be organized within the framework of *true* uniformitarianism, which is uniformity of natural law. It must realize that the story of earth history which it seeks to decipher has been one enacted within the framework of laws of conservation and decay, not of creation and development.

Therefore, to assume that the origin and history of the earth can be interpreted within the framework of an assumed uniformity of process rates and an assumed innate principle of evolutionary development is to reject the very basic laws of science which it professes to follow. But this would still be a permissible point of view to take, since not even uniformity of natural law can be *proved* in the prehistoric period. It is legitimate to assume, if one wishes to do so, that the two laws of thermodynamics were not in operation during the geological ages, and therefore that evolution and progress were possible on a worldwide scale. The paleontologic data can then be interpreted to fit into that framework if one wishes so to do. All the contradictions and anomalies which abound in such a system can all be explained away by piling hypothesis upon hypothesis (e.g., explaining great areas where "young" fossils are buried beneath "old" fossils by means of the theory of overthrust fault). Since all of this can never be subjected to laboratory verification, and is thus out of reach of the "scientific method," this framework of evolutionary uniformitarianism cannot be disproved scientifically.

But to say that a system erected upon such assumptions, which contradict the basic laws of science, is itself "scientific" is entirely unwarranted. And when the theory of evolution, based as it is upon this system, and the paleontologic data interpreted in accordance with it, is then made the foundation for all modern studies in theology, sociology, history, politics, and the arts — indeed into an all-embracing evolutionary world-view — and when all of this monstrous system is taught and indoctrinated as *scientific fact* almost everywhere, as it is today — the charge of *scientism* is a gross understatement of the true situation!

Implications of Evolution

The system of evolutionary uniformitarianism is, therefore, not a science but a system. It is a form of religion, a faith in innate progress, in materialistic development, in pantheistic humanism. It is the essence of modern man-centered culture. The evolutionary philosophy, as noted by Rene Dubos[25], has profoundly affected every field of human thought and activity. Man has been led to see himself as organically linked to all other forms of life:

> Comparative biology has revealed, furthermore, that man is linked to all living organisms through a common line of descent, and shares with them many characteristics of physicochemical constitution and of biological organization; the philosophical concept of the "great chain of being" can thus be restated now in the form of a scientific generalization.[26]

Not only so, but since all things can be explained in terms of this supposed universal process of evolution, effectuated by the cybernetic processes of mutation and natural selection, there is no need any longer to postulate a divine Creator originating or guiding the development of the universe. God becomes an unnecessary hypothesis. Man, as the highest stage of the evolutionary process, now having come to understand and even to guide it, is himself the creator.

> What is almost certain, however, is that the various components of human culture are now required not only for the survival of man, but also for his existential realization. Man created himself even as he created his culture and thereby he became dependent upon it.[27]

In the last analysis, then, evolution is a religion that permits man to divest himself of concern for or responsibility to a divine Creator. It is not a science in any proper sense of the word at all. And the same must therefore be true for the system of evolutionary historical geology which both supports it and is supported by it.

We hasten to say again that this is no criticism of the sciences of geology or biology, or of the scientists who practice them. The genuine sciences of geology and biology, dealing as they do with

---

[25]*Supra.*
[26]Dubos, *ibid,* p. x.
[27]*Ibid,* p. 8.

the *present* processes of the earth and of life are of highest merit and importance. It is believed that the great majority of geologists and biologists, who may nominally subscribe to the concept of evolution and the geological ages, have never fully considered its implications and that many of them would refute it if they did, professionally costly though such a stand might become.

It is not surprising, in view of the foregoing, that the system of evolution has been appropriated as the pseudo-scientific basis of every political or philosophical system of the past hundred years which has been opposed to Christianity, or even to theism in general. In particular this has been true of the various forms of modern "liberalism," including socialism, fascism and communism.

The influence of Darwinism upon Marxism has been especially significant:

> Orthodox Marxian socialists in the early years of the twentieth century felt quite at home in Darwinian surroundings. Karl Marx himself; with his belief in universal "dialectical" principles, had been as much a monist as Comte or Spencer. Reading *The Origin of Species* in 1860, he reported to Friedrich Engels, and later declared to Ferdinand LaSalle, that "Darwin's book is very important, and serves me as a basis in natural science for the class struggle in history." On the shelves of the socialist bookstores in Germany the works of Darwin and Marx stood side by side.[28]

The views of a prominent contemporary historian, Dean of the Graduate Faculties at Columbia University, are significant:

> It is a commonplace that Marx felt his own work to be the exact parallel of Darwin's. He even wished to dedicate a portion of *Das Kapital* to the author of *The Origin of Species*.[29]

Some of the reasons for this feeling of debt on the part of Marx are discussed as follows:

> It is that, like Darwin, Marx thought he had discovered the law of development. He saw history in stages, as the Darwinists saw geological strata and successive forms of life. . . . But there are even finer points of comparison. In keeping with the feelings of the age, both Marx and Darwin made struggle the means of development. Again, the measure of value in Darwin is survival with reproduc-

---

[28]Richard Hofstadter, *Social Darwinsim in American Thought* (New York: George Braziller, Inc., 1959), p. 115.
[29]Jacques Barzun, *Darwin, Marx, Wagner* (2nd. Ed., New York: Doubleday, 1958), p. 8.

tion — an absolute fact occurring in time and which wholly disregards the moral or esthetic quality of the product. In Marx the
measure of value is expended labor — an absolute fact occurring in
time, which also disregards the utility of the product.[30]

To similar effect is the definitive historical evaluation by Gertrude
Himmelfarb:

> There was truth in Engels' eulogy on Marx: "Just as Darwin dis-
> covered the law of evolution in organic nature, so Marx discovered
> the law of evolution in human history." What they both celebrated
> was the internal rhythm and course of life, the one the life of
> nature, the other of society, that proceeded by fixed laws, undis-
> tracted by the will of God or men. There were no catastrophes in
> history as there were none in nature. There were no inexplicable
> acts, no violations of the natural order. God was as powerless
> as individual men to interfere with the internal, self-adjusting
> dialectic of change and development.[31]

It is possible to trace similar direct connections between evolutionism and fascism, as well as other philosophical and political
symptoms of the basic antipathy to God which seems to afflict
a substantial segment of mankind. Perhaps of more immediate
concern is the fact that evolutionism is of predominant influence
in the system of John Dewey, the chief architect of modern edu-
cational theory in this country.

But that is another story, and would carry us too far afield
from the context of this study. Our point is simply that the
presently accepted system of evolutionary uniformitarianism in
the so-called historical geology has projected its influence deeply
into almost every sphere of human thought and that, in general,
this influence has been highly inimical to the cause of Biblical
Christianity. It is thus of immense concern to people in every
walk of life and cannot be left simply to the self-assumed authority
of those who claim jurisdiction over this field.

The Biblical Framework

The study of origins, destinies and meanings is thus properly
to be considered as outside the domain of science. Science deals
with present processes, and present processes are conservative
and degradational, not creative and organizational. Understanding

---

[30]*Ibid,* p. 170.
[31]*Darwin and the Darwinian Revolution* (London: Chatto & Windus,
    1959), p. 348.

of the creation and organization of the universe into its present form is therefore to be obtained from other sources than science. Religion necessarily enters the picture.

As noted, evolution is one such possible religious explanation for the universe. But as such, it explicitly contradicts what we know about the present world, which operates in accordance with the first and second laws of thermodynamics.

It is far more reasonable to recognize that neither the data nor the processes nor the methods of modern science can lead to an understanding of origins. And certainly, then, the unaided speculations of human reasonings cannot do it. Therefore, divine revelation is required if we are ever really to know anything about the Creation — its date, its duration, its methods, its order, or anything else about it.

It is eminently reasonable, therefore, to reorganize the data which we have obtained in our studies of the universe and its inhabitants in terms of the Biblical framework given us by divine revelation. The Biblical framework does give a perfectly satisfying system for harmonizing all the data of biology, geology, and paleontology, as well as other sciences.

The Bible record describes a special Creation of all things, fully functioning from the very beginning, complete and finished by creative and formative processes no longer in operation, now being sustained by God in accordance with the conservation principle enunciated in the first law of thermodynamics. It also described a fall of man, and God's curse pronounced on the earth, introducing a universal law of decay and disorder, in accordance with the second law of thermodynamics, which for the first time brought disharmony and death into the world. It then describes a great world-destroying Flood in the days of Noah, which completely changed the first cosmos and its structure and processes. It indicates, then, that since the Flood there has been an essential uniformity of both laws and processes, which can thus now be studied and elucidated by the scientific method.

It will be found, if enough study is devoted to it, that all the real data of the fossil record, of biological mechanisms, of geologic processes, and of all natural phenomena, can be oriented and understood within this framework. Such a system will be fully consistent with both the basic laws of science and history and the data of divine revelation.

Creationist Viewpoints

by John W. Klotz

JOHN W. KLOTZ

Dr. Klotz may be called a scientist or a theologian, for his daily work involves both fields of study. Professor of science at Concordia College, River Forest, Illinois, he is also pastor of Calvary Church, Wood Dale — perhaps the only active pastor currently listed in *American Men of Science*.

A 1941 graduate of Concordia Theological Seminary, he later received his Ph.D. from the University of Pittsburgh in the field of biology. His professional associations include membership in the Illinois Society for Medical Research, the Illinois Academy of Science, American Genetic Association, the American Association for the Advancement of Science, the National Biology Teachers Association.

Professor Klotz, a native of Pittsburgh, is well known among clergy and university groups as lecturer on evolution and the Bible. *Genes, Genesis and Evolution* is his first major publication.

II

CREATIONIST VIEWPOINTS

It all depends on your point of view. If you put a dot on a piece of paper and hold it about ten inches from your eyes you will have no difficulty in seeing it. If, however, you close one eye and move the paper back and forth, you will not be able to see the dot at one point. This is a demonstration of the well-known blind spot in the eye. Since the blind spot, which is due to the entry of the optic nerve, does not cover the same area in both eyes if you look at the dot with both eyes you can see it. But if you close one eye the dot falls on the blind spot of the eye which is open you do not see it. It all depends on your point of view. If you are looking with two eyes the spot is visible. If you look with only one eye the spot may not be seen.

So it is with the phenomena of nature. If you look with the eye of faith you see God in nature, both in creation and in preservation. But if you look only with the eye of reason and of cause and effect you may not see Him. This is why the creationist can see God while the man who does not look on the phenomena of nature with the same faith does not see Him there.

In teaching biology the creationist is concerned with demonstrating both creation and preservation. Both these doctrines, which are inherent in the First Article of the Apostle's Creed, are widely denied, not only by biologists but by most scientists today. Historically, it was the doctrine of preservation which first came under attack. Isaac Newton, pious Christian that he was, laid the foundation for attacks which were later made on the doctrine of preservation by developing the concept of the world as a machine and the picture of God as a watchmaker God. Newton believed that the age of miracles was past. He accepted the miracles of the Old Testament and of the New Testament. He believed that Jesus had arisen from the dead and looked upon his own work as a scientist as an opportunity to serve God. He believed, however, that God no longer worked through miracles but rather only through cause and effect relationships. He believed that the universe was an intricate machine and that the role of science was to discover the cause and effect relationships which governed it.

Newton was followed by a number of men, among whom was

35

LaPlace who believed that if there were a superhuman intelligence capable of knowing the position and momentum of every atom in the universe and capable of solving all mathematical equations, it could with precision state the minutest detail of every event whether it be thousands of years in the future or remote in the past. This was a natural deduction from the Newtonian picture of the world as a machine. Accordingly the role of science became that of seeking out the cause and effect relationships which govern the universe. With this point of view divine intervention receded farther and farther into the distance. It was not long until some scientists and philosophers of science applied Occam's razor to the system of Newton and LaPlace. They reasoned that God was no longer essential to the system. For all practical purposes it did not matter whether he existed or not, and in the course of time they gradually eliminated Him. This gave rise to the mechanism and materialism which characterized the science particularly of the eighteenth and nineteenth centuries.

It is interesting to note that God's role as the Preserver of the universe was denied before His role of Creator came under attack. Men were willing to assign Him the role of Creator if only He would back out of the picture and remain on the remote periphery. Only later did they begin to deny Him even this position. Newton and many of his followers had no difficulty with the doctrine of Creation. They were quite willing to believe that God created the universe which they saw; indeed they praised Him for His creation and saw in its intricacies His hand.

Newton's picture of the universe as a machine governed by strict cause and effect relationships has now been replaced, though the attacks on preservation continue. Today scientists no longer speak about strict cause and effect relationships. The indeterminism of Heisenberg, which holds in a physical sense only on the sub-atomic level, has had its influence also in the macrocosm. Today there is a great deal of debate still going on between those who are determinists, insisting that everything is fixed in the sense that Newton envisioned it, and the indeterminists who believe that it is not. Planck and Einstein are still determinists, arguing that the world is deterministic but that we cannot demonstrate this fact. Heisenberg and Eddington on the other hand, believe that the world is basically indeterministic.

Closely associated with the concept of God as the preserver of the universe is the concept of purpose in the universe and in what happens in the universe. We usually call this the concept of teleology. It, too, is an old concept and very much a common-sense concept. To anyone who looks with two eyes it is clear that there is purpose in the structure and function of living things and purpose in what happens in the lives of individuals, but if you close one eye, the idea of purpose is likely to disappear. Even the very ancient Greeks saw a pattern in the world about them and in the events of history. Later the Romans with their concept of law developed the idea of a plan. It was this Roman idea of a plan in creation and in the affairs of men which was taken over by the medievalists. They looked upon God as the law-giver. They believed that He had given the moral law, the ten commandments, to govern the activities of man in his social relationships, and they quickly drew the parallel of God as the law-giver in imposing the laws of nature on the created world. So the concept of a scientific law developed. It was believed that these were the laws issuing from the mind of the Creator which governed the activities of both the inorganic and the organic world. It was believed that what could be seen in the world was the evidence of God's plan for the world.

This idea of teleology, too, has come under attack and has been virtually rejected. Beck states that the arguments against teleology are decisive and most scientists today have denied entirely this concept of purpose (William S. Beck, *Modern Science and the Nature of Life*, New York: Harcourt, 1957, p. 180). For a time they even denied apparent purpose in the universe, arguing nothing ever appeared purposeful. Today they no longer do so. They are ready to admit apparent purpose in the universe, but they deny that it is really a part of a pattern or of a plan. Instead of teleology, Ernst Mayr suggests the word "teleonomy." He uses this term to designate apparent purpose in the biological world and he explains all apparent purpose on the basis of feed-back mechanisms. He believes that all instances of apparent purpose which we see in the natural world are due to these purposeless feedback mechanisms. He uses the analogy of the governor of an engine, of a thermostat, or of a guided missile that seeks out the airplane which it is to bring down. He tells us that all of these are instances of feedback and do not involve purposeful behavior. The governor of an engine does not really have as its purpose holding the speed of that engine at a certain point. There is nothing at all purposeful in its behavior. Centrifugal force shuts off the gas supply when a certain speed is reached and consequently the engine cannot operate at a higher rate. Similarly in a thermostat there is no real purpose in the action of the thermostat itself. An increase in temperature breaks the contact and shuts off the furnace. A decrease in temperature renews the contact and starts the furnace once more. The guided missile sends out radar waves and adjusts its course according to the pattern of the radar waves which it picks up. The course which it pursues is not at all purposeful: it is the result of a complicated feedback mechanism.

It might be noted that while there is no purpose in the action of the governor of an engine, or of a thermostat, or of a guided missile, there is purpose in the activity of the scientist and engineer who constructed these devices. The purpose may not be in the devices themselves but there certainly was purpose in the mind of the individual who devised them. And it is just this purpose that we creationists see in the universe.

It seems to me that the creationist teacher in approaching the phenomena of biology owes it to his pupils to point to the complexities of nature as an evidence of the wisdom of God and for His plan in nature. It also seems to me that the creationist teacher must point to instances of purpose in the lives of children and in the history of nations. Let me cover the second point first. I personally believe that there is purpose in everything that happens in my life, and I believe that there is purpose in all of history. My Lord tells me that not a sparrow falls from the heavens nor a hair from my head without His knowledge and will, and Paul assures me that all things work together for good to them who love God. There are many who would ridicule this sort of faith. It is probably true that in the past we Christians have erred in insisting that we could demonstrate the purpose in everything that happened in our own lives and also in the history of the world. This, I believe, is asking too much. I do not believe that I can demonstrate the purpose in every little event that happens in my life, but it is a matter of faith that I believe that even the little things have purpose. It is probably asking too much to see the hand of God in every event of history, but I believe, nevertheless, that it is there. What I am saying is this: that we must teach the children that God has a purpose in everything that happens in their lives and in the universe, even though they may not be able to demonstrate it. I am committed to the concept of teleology, and I have an obligation to bring others to that same commitment.

The concept of purpose, or teleology, is important not only to one's faith but also to the practice of that faith. If there is no purpose in the universe and if God has withdrawn completely from its governance, then there is no reason for prayer. Then James was wrong when he said prayer changes things. If the whole universe is a giant watch, remorselessly grinding our effects as the result of given causes, then man is indeed a helpless pawn of his environment and what is more important, God, Himself, cannot save him from the consequences of the cause and effect relationships which govern the universe. To be sure, God ordinarily works through cause and effect. But He is not bound by cause and effect as modern science seems to imply. Then, indeed, there is no point to pray because not even God can change things. Then, indeed, the pessimism which we see on so many sides today is justified.

Perhaps a word is in order about this pessimism, particularly on the part of scientists today. There was a day when the scientific world was very optimistic. Optimism can be traced through the history of science from its beginning in the sixteenth century down through the nineteenth century and even into the twentieth. This scientific optimism of the day is reflected in the many Utopian novels that were published during these centuries.

Today all this has changed and scientists are among the most pessimistic of human beings. They feel that man cannot be trusted with the power which modern science has given him. Perhaps the most pessimistic of all are the men who make up the Federation of Atomic Scientists. This pessimism is reflected in the anti-Utopian novels which are being written today. These include such novels as *1984, Brave New World,* and the like. These all picture a world dominated by science, but it is a very frightening world indeed.

As a matter of fact, only the Christian who believes that God is ruling this universe can afford to be an optimist today. If I did not believe that the future of this world was being determined in Heaven, I would be as pessimistic as most of my scientific colleagues. But I accept God's governance and because He is good I know He will bring about what is good for me and for my fellow Christians. God works through cause and effect relationships and as a scientist, it is these that I study. But He is not limited to cause and effect as I am.

What about the hand of God in the natural world? Let us turn our attention to this. As we look about us we cannot help but be impressed with the complexities of the living world. God has arranged it that the plant should turn toward the sun so that its leaves may receive an adequate amount of light. I know you can explain this on the basis of feedback mechanisms. I know that you can develop a mechanical explanation involving the synthesis of auxins, but I believe that behind this process is the hand of God. In a sense it is a feedback mechanism, but it is a feedback mechanism that has been developed with a purpose, just as the feedback mechanism in an engine or a thermostat or a guided missile has been developed with a purpose in mind. The creationist biology teacher is in a very good position to point to a great many of these adaptations. He will use the same adaptations which his non-creationist colleague uses but he will refer to them as evidence of the purposeful planning of God and not wonder at them as "marvels of evolutionary development."

Actually the intricacies of the universe are such that it is hard for any reasoning man to believe that they have developed by chance. I know the mechanistic biologist will argue that given enough time the impossible not only becomes possible but even probable. I know that the statistically minded biologist will argue that from a statistical standpoint these impossible situations are actually possible after all, that the so-called "laws of nature" are not absolute but are rather statements of a high degree of probability and that we must except exceptions even to these "laws of nature." It is these exceptions and not the hand of God which he believes accounts for these remarkable complexities.

Let me refer you though to some instances which I believe can be accounted for only by the purposeful planning of the Creator. The chemical compound most closely associated with life — water — is indeed a remarkable substance. We fail to appreciate it only because God has made it so abundant and we often take it for granted until we begin to be troubled by its lack.

The properties of water are in many ways unique. For one thing, it has a high heat-holding capacity. Compared with other substances, a larger quantity of heat is required to bring an increase in the temperature of a given quantity of water. It is for this reason that large quantities of water are used in air conditioning: water is an effective refrigerant. It can carry off large quantities of heat and have its temperature increased by only a few degrees. The amount of water on the earth's surface, estimated to be enough to form a layer over a mile deep if spread evenly over the earth's surface, tends to prevent sudden increases and decreases in temperature, as for example, between day and night. A rock, for instance, is very hot during the day and very cold at night. The change in temperature in a body of water is by comparison insignificant. The presence of large quantities of water in the oceans and the Great Lakes is responsible for the fact that coastal cities are not as warm in summer or as cold in winter as are inland areas: they have a natural air conditioning. Not only does the temperature of a body of water itself remain relatively constant, but the atmosphere in its immediate vicinity is also affected. This high heat-holding capacity of water also prevents the occurrence of catastrophic ocean currents and winds which might otherwise result from sudden changes in temperature.

Another important property of water is the large amount of heat that is necessary to change it from a solid or a liquid state to a vapor state. To change water from a liquid to a gaseous state (and this occurs at all temperatures, not only at the boiling point) requires from 500 to 600 calories per gram. Condensation transfers that same amount of heat from the water to its environment. This is particularly important in cooling plants and animals. Because vaporization of water removes large quantities of heat, perspiration is an effective cooling agent in animals. Transpiration, the evaporation of water from leaves, brings the same result in plants. This is important because the upper practical limits of life are reached at about 104° F. Few plants and animals can be active and some cannot even live above this temperature. Both plants and animals are frequently exposed to situations where the absorption of heat might easily raise their temperatures above this point were it not for perspiration and transpiration.

Water also gives up a large quantity of heat when it freezes. In freezing it may actually increase the temperature of the surrounding atmosphere. Taken together, these two characteristics of water make possible the exchange of large quantities of heat between the tropics and the polar regions. As water vaporizes in the tropics it removes a great deal of heat from these regions, and when it cools and condenses in the colder regions it gives off this heat. Later when it changes from a liquid to a solid state it releases a further quantity of heat. This process is reversed when the ice and snow melt and when the water vaporizes once more. The whole cycle results in a more uniform temperature over the surface of the earth and makes possible life as we know it. If we were subjected to extremes of temperature, life would be a very precarious thing.

A very unusual property of water is the fact that it reaches its greatest density at about 39° F, that is, at this point it is heaviest. Most liquids become denser as they cool and reach their greatest density at the freezing point. Yet water is almost unique in this respect, and this property is an important one. It keeps water from freezing from the bottom up since water at the freezing point is lighter than water at 39° F. and tends to rise to the surface. In this way freezing begins at the surface and the bottom freezes last. In many cases the water at the bottom of the pond never freezes, and thus organisms living there are at least somewhat protected.

This property of water is also important in the melting of water in the spring. Water is a poor conductor of heat and if streams froze over from the bottom and melted from the top they would melt very slowly. The water forming on the top of such a melting stream might well act as an insulator, preventing the ice underneath from being affected by the sun's rays. However, as water melts it sinks to the bottom so that the ice is always formed at the top where it can absorb the direct rays of the sun.

This property of water is also important in supplying oxygen to ponds and lakes. Water at the surface is relatively well supplied with oxygen; water at the bottom tends to be deficient in oxygen. As the pond cools in the fall and winter the oxygen-rich water on the surface tends to sink and to replace the oxygen-deficient water at the bottom. As the temperature decreases and nears the freezing point, the water which is now at the bottom moves once more to the top where it again comes into contact with oxygen. In the spring the water produced by melting ice moves from the top where it has gathered oxygen to the bottom. Then as it becomes still warmer it moves to the top once more. Thus the oxygen-rich water at the surface is moved repeatedly to the bottom of the pond.

Another point to be considered is the greenhouse effect, brought about by the presence of water vapor in the atmosphere. A greenhouse maintains a higher temperature than the surrounding environment because glass permits sunlight to pass in freely but absorbs and reflects many of the longer heat rays remitted by objects in the greenhouse. Water vapor in the atmosphere does much the same thing. The sunlight is permitted to pass through freely, but many of the longer heat rays re-emitted by the earth are absorbed and reflected back to earth. This prevents extreme variations in temperature between night and day.

Still another property of water is that it is the "universal" solvent. Fortunately not all substances are soluble in water; otherwise it would not be possible to find a container for water. But more substances are soluble in water than in any other solvent, and many substances which will not dissolve will form a colloidal suspension with water. Substances in solution or in colloidal suspension react much more quickly than substances that are not. It is probable that all chemical reactions of living protoplasm take place between substances in solution or in colloidal suspension.

It is hard to believe that this unique collection of properties should have arisen by chance. One might expect a single unusual property in one substance but it is hard to believe that this aggregation developed by chance. It is far more plausible to believe that this is an evidence of the plan of God. He gave water the properties that it has because He was designing it for specific purposes in serving living things.

Another unusual substance associated with living things is protein. It might be said that this chemical compound is the characteristic compound of living things. Its unusual characteristic is its complexity. Proteins are the most complex compounds known with molecular weights in the hundreds of thousands. Only recently have we succeeded in synthesizing proteins in the laboratory. They are characteristic of the species, that is, dog protein is never found in human beings and vice versa. It may well be that no two human beings have the same proteins unless they are identical twins. This seems to account for the fact that skin grafts, bone grafts, artery grafts and the like do not "take" permanently but merely serve as the scaffolding around which the individual builds his own tissues. It is hard to believe that such a type of chemical substance could have arisen by chance. Blum calculates that the chance of forming a polypeptid — one of the precursors of protein — of only ten amino acid units would be something like 0.00000000000000000001. Such a polypeptid would still be very small. After the polypeptid stage is reached the proteose stage must be reached and only after this can the protein stage be reached. Blum says further that the formation of a polypeptid of the size of the smallest known protein seems beyond all probability (Harold F. Blum, *Time's Arrow and Evolution*, Princeton University Press, 1951, p. 163).

Also interesting are the various obligate relationships. One of the best known of these is the relationship of the yucca moth and the yucca plant, or Spanish bayonet. The yucca flower hangs down and the pistil or female part of the flower is lower than the stamens or male parts. However the stigma, the part of the flower specialized for the reception of pollen is cup-shaped and so arranged that it is impossible for the pollen to fall onto it. Instead the pollen must be transported by the female of the yucca moth, which begins her work soon after sunset. She collects a quantity of pollen from the stamens of the plant and holds it in her specially constructed mouth parts. Then she flies to another yucca flower, pierces the ovary with her ovipositor, and after laying one or more eggs creeps down the style and stuffs the ball of pollen into the stigma. The plant produces a large number of seeds. Some are eaten by the larvae of the moth and some mature to perpetuate the plant.

This relationship is absolutely essential for both the yucca plant and the yucca moth. The range of one is limited by the other.

It is hard to believe that this sort of relationship could have developed by chance.

We can further evidence of the wisdom of God in the many instances where man to his regret has attempted to improve on the balance of nature which God has established, only to upset it.

When the early settlers came to Australia, they found there no placental mammals except the dingo or wild dog and a few species of rodents. Coming from Europe as they did, they remembered the fine hunting provided by the rabbit there. And so, in an attempt to improve on nature, Thomas Austin imported some twenty-four European rabbits in 1859. The result was unfortunate, for there were no natural enemies in Australia to keep the rabbits in check. They multiplied beyond all expectation and did serious damage, destroying the grass on which the sheep fed. At first an attempt was made to control them by building a rabbit proof fence across the continent in Queensland, but this proved useless for the rabbits got through it. Then an attempt was made to reduce their numbers by a system of bounties but again this effort proved unsuccessful. Only in recent years has a solution been found, and that is an introduction of a virus disease, myxomatosis, which kills the rabbits and keeps their number in check. Even this may not be the final answer, for we are now beginning to hear of virus resistant rabbits in Australia. But the present reduction in their numbers has brought about great benefits. Rangeland, once ravaged by erosion and hills grazed to the soil for decades are now miraculously clothed in green.

It is not uncommon that interference with nature to solve one problem will raise others. Such has been the case in the various drainage projects intended to increase the amount of land available for agricultural purposes and also to decrease the number of mosquitoes by decreasing their breeding grounds. But this same procedure which alleviates the mosquito nuisance and adds to our agricultural potential also decreases the number of ducks, for these ponds and marshes are their breeding grounds. Formerly ducks bred throughout the upper Mississippi Valley; today, because of the drainage of swamps and ponds, very few ducks breed in the United States; breeding is restricted almost entirely to Canada.

Another example of this same problem is to be seen in the present situation in Colorado. The ranchers of the Toponas district there, wishing to save their cattle, carried out a campaign to exterminate the coyotes that were attacking the lambs and young calves. The coyotes disappeared, but the ranchers noticed that their pasture land was no longer able to support as many animals as before. The reason was that with nothing to stop them, rabbits, gophers and other rodents began to attack the meadows. Now the ranchers are encouraging the coyotes to breed.

A similar problem exists in the use of pesticides and herbicides today. The vast majority of plant-feeding insects throughout the world are in a satisfactory natural balance, and this is true also of various weeds. Insecticides are necessary only when effective, beneficial organisms, or other natural control factors, are either lacking or are unable to maintain the pest species below a level of economic importance. But DDT is effective not only against mosquitoes and flies; it also kills honey bees, other useful insects, and birds. Its extensive use might actually reduce the fruit crop in a given area to a marked degree and upset the balance of nature in other ways. We have a number of instances in which even human deaths have been traced to pesticide poisoning. There is no doubt that the number of useful plants and animals has been reduced by the extensive use of herbicides and pesticides. No doubt they are necessary in the present stage of agricultural development but they ought to be used with discrimination. Meanwhile every effort should be made to study and utilize natural controls.

The gypsy moth was imported into the United States in 1886. It was hoped that by using this moth a native silk industry could be established. Accidentally, the moth escaped, and the moth has proved to be a serious pest. It feeds especially on native shade trees. Literally millions of acres of trees in New England have been defoliated by this pest and millions of dollars have been spent by state and federal governments in an attempt to control it.

Actually in most cases nature maintains a good balance so long as man does not interfere, and in interfering he is more likely to do harm than good. It is this point which we want to bring out in teaching our children. As Christians we cannot help but be impressed with the wisdom of God in setting up the natural world nor can we fail to emphasize plan and purpose in the world about us.

The other area in which creationist teaching will be different is in the matter of evolution. I believe that it is very necessary to discuss this topic with our pupils. It cannot be ignored: indeed it must be dealt with carefully and in detail. It is most important that we discuss this topic with our pupils lest they meet it later on and believe that we are totally ignorant of the subject.

It is obvious that the currently accepted picture of creation is as different from the Biblical account as is the currently accepted picture of preservation. And it is because of the same approach that the scientific picture of creation is different. In other words, evolution represents the application of Newtonian mechanics to the account of origins. It was inevitable that such a theory should develop: indeed it is almost strange that a well-developed modern theory of evolution had to wait until about two hundred years ago. Historians of science usually account for this on the basis that the men of the Renaissance looked up to the civilization of the Greeks and Romans, regarding them as much more highly developed than their own. They found it difficult to accept the idea of progress which is implicit in the theory of evolution, and it was only toward the middle of the nineteenth century that they began to consider the possibility of development and progress.

As I said, it was inevitable that a theory of evolution should have developed. If Darwin had not come to these conclusions, someone else would have. Extrapolating from the mechanical concept of the operation of the universe inevitably led to a mechanical concept of the origin of the universe. In a way it is almost surprising that more furor should be stirred up by the scientific theories of the origin of the universe than has been stirred up by scientific theories of the current operation of the universe.

It seems to me that as creationists we must deal with the current theories of evolution. I believe it is important to approach this from an historical standpoint. Perhaps it would be well as much as possible to deal not only with the history of the theory of evolution but with the history of science itself. I believe it is important that we should lead our students to recognize the changing points of view which are inevitably a part of science. Too often people have a two-dimensional picture of science. They come to regard the currently accepted theories of science as the last word. Any knowledgeable scientist will tell you that the history of science is a history of change. Schwab of the University of Chicago says that the duration of a revisionary cycle in a median science is fifteen years. He says that in that time the body of knowledge becomes as obsolete as the notion of body humors (*The Science Teacher*, 27:7). Oppenheimer says much the same thing (*Science Teacher*, 28:31).

In this connection it might be well for each of us to read "Cognitive Dissonance" by E. G. Boring, Professor Emeritus of Psychology at Harvard. The article appeared in 1964 in *Science* (145:680-5). He calls attention to the necessary lack of certainty in science and speaks of the changing paradigms in science.

These are essentially fundamental hypotheses or points of view. A change in a scientific paradigm results, according to Boring, in a scientific revolution. He cites the geocentric theory of Ptolemy as an example of a paradigm which was supplanted by the heliocentric system of Copernicus. He speaks of the creationist point of view as one paradigm and evolution as another paradigm. These are fundamental to the thinking of men until something better comes along. They work best for the time being and their influence is profound. However, they are not permanent, and inevitably they are replaced by another paradigm.

Another term that Boring uses is "egoism" which he believes is the generator of dissonance between pride and objectivity. He believes, and most historians of science will agree with him, that scientists cling tenaciously to conceptual schemes even in the light of mounting evidence against them. The very lifeblood of scientific progress is change: to deny this is to deny science. Yet scientists form an emotional attachment to the hypotheses and theories which they have come to accept. There is a pride of authorship, a fierce loyalty to the conceptual scheme which the individual has espoused. The longevity of a pet theory is directly proportional to the hero status of its proponent: yet in the course of time, all conceptual schemes are doomed either to be. modified or replaced completely.

It seems to me that when we recognize these general characteristics of science, we come up with something quite different than the generally accepted picture that modern science represents the last word and that those who do not agree with the currently accepted paradigm are obviously benighted and hopeless obscurantists.

Some will argue that while scientific points of view change, they never return to a point of view which has been rejected by science. This is in keeping with the currently-accepted picture of science constantly moving forward even though its progress may be temporarily stymied. Yet as a matter of fact, science sometimes moves backward, rejecting theories which later proved to be correct. For instance, Aristarchus of Samos living in 281 B.C. suggested a heliocentric system which was very similar to the Copernican system. He recognized that the sun was much farther from the earth than the moon, and he believed that the distance of the fixed stars from the sun was immensely great as compared with that of the earth. Yet this heliocentric theory of Aristarchus was rejected in favor of the geocentric theory developed by Aristotle and worked out in detail by Ptolemy in the second century A.D.

Another example is the rejection of epigenesis by Swammerdam in the seventeenth century in favor of a theory of preformation which was in turn replaced once more by the currently accepted theory of epigenesis. The Greeks accepted the theory of epigenesis, the idea that the organism gradually develops or unfolds in embryonic life. This theory continued to be accepted through Roman times and the Middle Ages. Harvey, who is best known for his studies of the circulation of the blood, did some work in embryology and also accepted the theory of epigenesis. The early microscopists developed some fantastic theories as a result of their studies. One of these was the preformation theory of Swammerdam, who believed that he was able to see a fully formed human being in each sperm. This idea was generally accepted for about a hundred years until epigenesis was reintroduced by Wolff. Our modern theories of embryonic development are essentially those of Caspar Wolff whose ideas represented a return to the rejected theories of Aristotle and Harvey.

There is something else that deserves to be said in this connection, and that is this: there is no disagreement between creationists and evolutionists on the observed facts. We accept the same empirical data. The difference comes in the way in which we organize these data into a conceptual scheme. In other words, we are following different paradigms. It is not unusual for people to agree on the observed facts and yet to follow different paradigms. This was the case when Copernicus developed his theory. He had essentially the same observational data with which Ptolemy worked: the only change was that Copernicus looked at it from a different point of view. Only after the telescope was developed, a hundred years later, was there additional observational data available, and these data fitted better the heliocentric paradigm than the geocentric paradigm.

Now what shall we say about evolution? First of all, I believe that we must avoid all emotionalism in discussing the topic. This is difficult to do but we must recognize that some of the tensions which exist between creationists and evolutionists are due to the poor judgment which some early apologists of the Scriptures used. In any objective discussion there is no place for the *argumentum ad hominem* and there is no place for personal attacks.

Secondly, I believe that we must recognize that our point of view is based ultimately on faith. It is a mistake to base creationism on empirical observations. The very nature of the problem does not lend itself to this, since the experimental method, the genius of modern science, has very little use in the study of evolution. Our opposition to evolution is based on our acceptance of the Bible as God's Word. We believe that the Genesis account is a factual account: we insist that God is communicating history to us here. There are many reasons for taking this point of view. Our Saviour accepts Genesis as an historical account, referring to both the first and second chapter in his controversy with the Pharisees over marriage and divorce. It is hard to believe that Jesus accommodated Himself to the erroneous opinion of his contemporaries if this is not an historical account and it is even harder to believe that He was Himself deceived as to the nature of this account.

Even more striking are Paul's references to the creation story. He speaks of one Adam and one Christ in Romans 5, and I Corinthians 15. According to evolutionary theory, it is impossible for the human race to have descended from a single Adam. Adam and Eve cannot represent individuals: they must represent an evolutionary population, yet Paul speaks of one Adam, and if Adam stands for a group of people then Christ may also stand for a group of people.

In I Corinthians 11, Paul once more refers to the story of creation. Here he specifically says that woman was taken out of the man (verse 8 — original Greek). In I Timothy 2:13, he says Adam was formed first and then Eve, and goes on to say Adam was not deceived, but the woman was deceived. If one would argue that Adam and Eve stand for evolutionary populations one would have to insist that for a time the species *Homo sapiens* consisted solely of males and that females developed only later, which is biological nonsense.

Interpreting Genesis as an historical account has been the traditional Protestant approach. Luther and his contemporaries were much concerned with the allegorical interpretation which was current in the Middle Ages. It is a strange situation that those who would claim to be modern today are returning to an old interpretation which the Reformers found wanting and abandoned. Perhaps we have an example here of a rejected paradigm being resurrected.

The hazards of a consistent application of this principle of interpretation must also be pointed out. If Genesis is not historical, it is easy to argue that the Bible and science are talking about two different things. It is not long until this principle is applied not only to the miracles of the Old and New Testaments but also the greatest miracle of them all, the resurrection of Jesus Christ from the dead. Scientific humanism, the religion of so many men and women today, is the inevitable consequence. None of the leading evolutionary theorists today are Christians. Please note I am not denying the Christianity of many sincere men who accept the theory of evolution: what I am saying is, that the men who are in the forefront, shaping and modifying current evolutionary theory are, to the best of my knowledge, all humanists. Pierre Teilhard de Chardin, it is true, was a Jesuit, but he worked in a very limited area of the evolutionary theory, the history of man's evolutionary development. Julian Huxley, one of the leading British evolutionists, does not hesitate to speak of the decline and disappearance of the God concept. Simpson regards Christianity as "higher superstition," and believes that it will inevitably be replaced by evolutionary humanism which rejects the idea of God and is totally man-oriented. Bishop Robinson in his *Honest to God* also represents this point of view.

What I am saying is this: that I believe we should point out to our pupils that acceptance of the Biblical account is based on faith and we should attempt to have them approach evolution from this standpoint. The fact of the matter is that there are some observational data which point strongly in the direction of the type of change which the evolutionist postulates and there are other data which do not fit the theory of evolution. This is not at all strange: Boring refers to it as dissonance which he says results when there is not enough evidence to resolve a 50-50 decision. He says that to remain healthy and to cope with this dissonance one alters the 50-50 alternative to a 60-40 and acts on the 60. Resolution of the difficulty results from pushing the contradiction aside and refusing to worry about it. Boring believes that this occurs continually and that such resolutions of dissonance are almost inescapable. Personally, I suspect that this is what has happened in the theory of evolution.

To me the two greatest problem areas are the fossils and the geographical distribution of plants and animals. If I look at the data objectively I am forced to conclude that they support evolution rather than special creation. I know there are problems involved: I know for instance as Hamon points out, that the entire paleontological record is a 400 page novel in which we have pages 13, 38, 170, 172, 173, 340 and 400 and from these we are trying to construct the whole story (J. Hill Hamon, "Fossil Hunting in the Indiana Coal Measures," *Outdoor Indiana,* March 1964, p. 27 f.). I also know that the evolutionist has some major problems in explaining the fossil record, but I believe you and I have more problems with the fossils than he does.

So far as the record of geographical distribution is concerned, I cannot explain the limited range of some organisms on the basis of special creation. I know that the evolutionist, also, has some problems in this area, but I believe that viewed objectively the evidence supports evolution rather than special creation.

On the other hand, I believe that the evolutionist has a major problem in describing the mechanism of evolution and also in presenting a reasonable picture of the stages of human evolution. It is simply a fact that we do not have a satisfactory mechanism for change of the degree required by the theory of evolution. By far, the vast majority of mutations are lethal. Winchester, Glass, and H. J. Muller are all agreed that over 99 per cent of all mutations that have been studied are harmful in some degree: (Albert M. Winchester *Genetics,* Boston: Houghton-Mifflin, 1951 p. 290; Bentley Glass "The Genetic Hazards of Radiation" *Science* 126, 1957, 243; H. J. Muller "Genetic Damage Produced by Radiation" *Science* 121, 1955, 837).

It is hard to believe that this mechanism would provide adequately for the change needed in evolution. Evolutionists argue that natural selection operates with the less than 1 per cent of mutations which are neutral or harmful. This is possible, but it would slow down substantially the rate of evolution requiring literally an eternity of time to make possible the degree of change which is needed in the development of living things.

The only other mechanism available to the evolutionist is chromosomal change. These are less common than mutations and are even more likely to be harmful. It is simply a fact that we do not know any mechanism which would provide change of the degree needed for progressive evolution.

In this connection it is interesting to note the concern which evolutionists feel for any increase in man-made radiation. Increased radiation means an increase in the mutation rate. If this were the mechanism whereby progressive evolution occurred and if the path of evolution ultimately was one of improvement then anything which would speed up the rate of mutation, such as radiation, would be regarded as favorable, but the fact of the matter is it is regarded as undesirable and very much unfavorable. Here is a tacit recognition that mutation is not an adequate mechanism for evolution.

The story of human evolution is far from a satisfactory one. While there are a great many fossils of plants and animals, the number of human fossils is relatively small, and this creates a problem for the evolutionist. He usually explains the paucity of fossils by the practice of earth burial which he believes began very early in man's history. I am inclined to agree with him: I look upon this, though, as evidence of man's early recognition of the doctrine of the resurrection, so that he had respect for his dead and did not permit them to lie where they fell.

In any case, we do not have very many fossils of prehistoric man. Those that we have are classified by almost all workers in the genus *Homo*. By this classification the evolutionist is saying that the forms he has are not substantially different than human beings which are alive today. Indeed many of the so-called prehistoric human beings are now recognized to be members of the species *Homo sapiens*. This is true of the Neanderthal man (the cave man) and of Cro-Magnon. The story of human evolution, as intensively as it has been investigated, still does not give the information that the evolutionist is looking for.

I believe that the creationist teacher will want to tell his pupils about currently accepted theories of evolution and will want to present objectively the evidences for evolution as they exist. In addition he will want to show the many weaknesses of the current theory of evolution. He will want to point out to his pupils the limitations which the restricted evidence we have imposes. He will also want to call attention to the limitations imposed by the impossibility of any extensive experimentation. He will want to call attention to the fact that evolution is a scientific paradigm and that scientific paradigms usually are replaced or modified. In the light of all of this he will ask his pupils to reserve judgment on the scientific aspects of the theory while clinging closely by faith to the Biblical Genesis account. This is not so unreasonable after all.

Can We Accept Theistic Evolution?
by Paul A. Zimmerman

PAUL A. ZIMMERMAN

Dr. Zimmerman became the first president of Concordia Lutheran Junior College, Ann Arbor, Michigan, in 1961; it opened in 1963. He is a graduate of Concordia College, Fort Wayne, Indiana (1939), and of Concordia Seminary, St. Louis, Missouri (B.A., 1941; B.D., 1944). He received his M.A. degree in education from the University of Illinois in 1947, and his Ph.D. in chemistry from the same institution in 1951.

Before coming to Ann Arbor, Dr. Zimmerman was professor of science and religion at Bethany Lutheran College, Mankato, Minnesota. He also served as professor of science and religion at Concordia Teachers College, Seward, Nebraska. In 1954, he became president of that institution and served until coming to Michigan in 1961.

Dr. Zimmerman has contributed to both theological and scientific publications. He is particularly interested in problems involving the relationship of science and the Bible. He has published articles in *The Concordia Theological Monthly, The Lutheran Witness, Lutheran Education, The Cresset,* and *The Journal of the American Chemical Society.* In 1959, he served as editor and co-author of the volume *Darwin, Evolution and Creation.*

III

CAN WE ACCEPT THEISTIC EVOLUTION?

There are many ways in which one might approach the task assigned to this essayist. Perhaps the best way at this point in time would be to simply ask the question, "Can we accept theistic evolution?" then to attempt to answer the question using a theological approach. There is no need to delineate here the reasons why this question is being asked in the situation in which it is being discussed these days. Pressures from our scientific culture and outlook have pressed in upon our theological world expressing real concerns and sometimes going so far as to demand that theology be directed by science. It is often said, "In the light of modern science, the early chapters of Genesis simply can no longer be regarded as literal history or literal science."

The problem actually is broader in the sense that the naturalism which is a part of the thinking of so many in our day pressures theology to eradicate all supernaturalism from the Bible. Thus you find not only the early chapters of Genesis being questioned, but the miracles recorded in both the Old and New Testaments. C. S. Lewis, in his book on miracles (*Miracles*, New York: Macmillan Co., 1947, p. 12) states, "The result of our historical inquiries thus depends on the philosophical views which we have been holding before we begin to look at the evidence. The philosophical question must therefore come first." Lewis goes on to give an example in which an author states that the Gospel of John must have been written after the execution of Peter because in the fourth Gospel Christ is represented as predicting the execution of Peter. Lewis comments that the author has assumed that real predictions of a prophetic nature could never occur. Lewis scores him for having done this without having spelled out a presupposition which he never communicates to his reader. He says, "He has brought his disbelief in predictions to his historical work, so to speak, ready made."

Perhaps this illustration will serve to point out that before one can achieve an answer to the theological question which we have asked, one must decide whether or not he is going to choose as his philosophical bias pure naturalism or supernaturalism. If naturalism is his choice, then obviously there is no point in having a discussion. If supernaturalism is his choice, then he must play by the rules of the game in accord with what we have been prone to call sound hermeneutics.

As to presuppositions for this paper in answering the basic questions and the satellite questions connected with it, we would abide by the following rubrics: The questions concerning the language of the text in Genesis must be determined by: 1. The decision must grow out of the text. 2. It must be in harmony with the context. 3. It must not contradict any clear passage of Scripture or any article of faith, particularly the doctrine of law and gospel (Romans 5:12-19). No interpretation dare be employed which undermines the certainty that the text is in every word the Word of God, or which is out of harmony with the confessions of the church.

Definitions

Another introductory consideration has to do with definitions and the delineation of areas of first concern. Let us take definitions first. By "evolution" we mean the complete theory of evolution from the so-called first gaseous plasma which is said to have preceded the formation of the elements down to man. By "theistic evolution" we mean that instead of this being governed by the rules of chance and natural selection, as held by evolutionists, that the process is directed by God.

By "creation" we mean that God originally created certain "kinds" in the beginning of the world's history. We are not told specifically what are included in the "kinds" with the exception of man who is mentioned on the sixth day. The use of the term "kind" in Leviticus 11, however, makes quite clear that it is a term larger than species, perhaps being large enough in some instances to include a family or order. It is not possible to define precisely how the term is used in Genesis 1 so far as the exact limits of the category "kind." That there are limits is clear in the text from the constant repetition of the phrase that things reproduce "after their kind." This does not rule out variation or even the possibility of the origin of new species or new genera. It would rule out the production of new "kinds." Thus it would rule out the production of a new kind, such as, man from a lower form of life.

Another preliminary item deals with the question of "time." Actually the age of the earth does not lie at the heart of the problem. A great age for the earth is a vital requirement for the evolutionist; it is much less important for the creationist. The evolutionist needs it for new forms to develop. The creationists do not.

Neither do I have the time to go into an extensive treatment of the word "yom" which is translated "day" in Genesis 1. I cannot pass it by, however, without a few general remarks which could be expanded in the discussion once the main topic has been adequately treated. These considerations may be listed in tabular form as follows:

1. We do not understand either theologically or scientifically the essence of "time."

2. We are dealing with an account of the origin of all things in which "time" as well as "space" is in the process of being created. This alone may rule out any common sense notions or scientific notions we have of "time" today.

3. I would agree with Edward Young who says, "The six days are to be understood in a chronological sense, that is, one day following another in succession. This fact is emphasized in that the days are designated, one, two, three, etc." (*Westminster Theological Journal*, May, 1963, p. 169)

4. The creation days are best designated as just that — *creation days*.

5. The text does not give us the length of the days. The constant repetition of the formula "evening and morning" which is associated in verse 3 with light and darkness, points forcibly, however, to a day governed by a succession of light and darkness. Nevertheless, W. M. Oesch has pointed out that the "Christian church has nowhere dogmatized the present measurement of time (24 hours) for these days. For that purpose the anomalies of the first and seventh days are simply too great." (*Lutherischer Rundblick*, May 1, 1960, pp. 53-92) Oesch asserts that there is a question whether or not the time of the spirit sweeping over the "deep" is to be included in the first day. Originally there was darkness. Then God created light. This light is called "day." Then comes evening and then comes morning — "first day." There is a succession of darkness and light followed by darkness and light indicating that the first day may follow the activity of the spirit over the deep. Oesch also recognizes as do other commentators that the first three days were not solar days such as we now have, inasmuch as the sun, moon, and stars had not yet been made. Some, however, think that the activity of the fourth day was a clearing up of the fact that these heavenly bodies had been placed there previously.

Oesch also points to the fact that there is no close of the seventh day. However, I have never been impressed by this, inasmuch as there was no creative activity on this day. It merely marks the time of God's bringing to a close the work that he had been doing and the initiation of his overall continual work of providence.

The sainted George V. Schick and Walter A. Maier, professors of Hebrew at Concordia Seminary, St. Louis, Missouri, consistently held that the text supported the idea of an ordinary day, particularly in view of Exodus 20 and 33 where the Sabbath rule is established. The modern *Interpreter's Bible* agrees and states: "There can be no question but that by 'day' the author means just what we mean — the time required for one revolution of the earth on its axis. Had he meant an aeon he would certainly, in view of his fondness for numbers, have stated the number of millennium each period embraces" (*Interpreter's Bible*, Vol. I, New York: Abingdon Cokesbury Press, 1952, p. 417).

The attempting to stretch the days out to long periods of time generally is unsuccessful in bringing about the desired harmonization of Genesis 1 with geology.

One would like to dwell on this intriguing topic, but as I have indicated earlier, it does not get us to the heart of the problem. The real question is, "Can we accept the evolution of man from a lower form of life?" It is this question that we should now like to approach.

Does the Sacred Text Indicate Evolution?

We cannot make any progress in answering the question until we decide whether or not Genesis is patently unscientific. By this I do not mean to deal with the question of whether or not it is a scientific textbook. This red herring ought to be buried permanently. The question rather is, "Does it contain information which is correct in substance?" Bernard Ramm, the Baptist scholar, said it well when he stated that "religion is not pure spirit, pure eternal fact. The evangelical faith has doctrines which directly pertain to the world of fact. The verse which opens the canon of sacred scriptures refers to nature, namely its creation by Almighty God. The incarnation and resurrection are in the stream of history" (Bernard Ramm, *The Christian View of Science and Scripture*, Grand Rapids, Michigan: William B. Eerdmans, 1954, p. 38).

There are some who attempt to persuade us that the Bible contains the world view of the ancient Jews which might be described somewhat as follows. "In Scripture that flat earth is founded upon an underlying sea; it is stationary; the heavens are like an upturned bowl or canopy above it; the circumference of this ball rests on pillars; the sun, moon, and stars move within this firmament of special purpose to illumine man; there is a sea above the sky; the waters which were above the heavens and through the windows of heaven the rain comes down; within the earth is sheol, where dwell the shadowy dead; this whole cosmic system is suspended over vacancy; and it as all made in six days with the morning and evening a short measurable time before."

Statements like this are repeated so often that we finally begin to believe them even though they are not based on Scripture's teaching. C. Gaenssle, in the *Concordia Theological Monthly,* 1942, pages 738-749, marshals Biblical evidence to show that Scripture does not teach such a cosmology. Gaenssle cites passages such as Isaiah 40:22, Psalm 104:2 and Isaiah 34:4 in which the heavens are referred to as being stretched out like a curtain, like a tent, and as being due to be rolled up at the end of time like a scroll. Ramm asks, "Can anyone with these texts before him seriously, honestly believe that the writers of the words entertained the crude, inept notion of a metallic canopy over their heads?" (op. cit.) With reference to the seas he concludes, "Consequently, when the earth is said to be founded on the seas and spread out upon the waters, there is no reason to assume that the psalmist is singing of an invisible ocean on which the earth rests or is spread out, but only of earthly waters on which the earth touches and over which it is elevated." Ramm quotes Gaenssle with reference to the Hebrew word "tehom"; "The upper terrestrial ocean satisfies all requirements, and it lies below or beneath in the same sense as the Dead Sea lies under Mount Pisgah, the land of Moab." Ramm also adds that the pillars of the earth mentioned in Job 9:6 are the rocks which bear up the surface of the earth.

It is interesting that the English physicist, Frederick A. Filby takes the same position regarding the word for the atmosphere which is actually mistranslated as "firmament." He says, "the original idea behind the Hebrew word 'raqiya' (firmament) seems to be the process of beating or stamping out. With the development of language this has led to two distinct meanings. If clay in a mold is stamped on, it will become compressed, firmer, more solid . . . however, the word 'raqiya' was connected with a second and much commoner conception. If gold or silver was beaten or stamped on, it became very thin. The ancients were in fact very good at this process and specimens of their work show they used gold leaf down to 1/5000 of an inch thick. The word thus acquired the meaning of expanse and of thinness and we find this born out in related expressions such as the word 'raq' used for Pharaoh's thin kine and 'raquiq' used for wafers" (*Creation Revealed*, 1964, Scotland: Pickering & Inglis, p. 72). Filby goes on to point out that this description of the expanse beyond the earth of the atmosphere and outer space beyond it is a really very accurate one. We ought not pass this point without remembering that not so many years ago the concept of creatio ex nihilo (creation out of nothing) was regarded as being most unscientific. This was before the discovery that energy and matter are convertible. I am not attempting to demonstrate that the Bible can be used as any kind of a scientific textbook. I am saying, however, that where we have been patient enough to study it thoroughly and also from time to time to progress in our concept of nature that we have not found the Bible wanting. We need more patience and ought not fall into the snare of declaring the Bible to be in error because we cannot solve all of the difficulties that presently face us.

What Type of Literature?

In asking whether or not theistic evolution may be found in the text, we must also come to grips with the question as to what kind of literature we have in Genesis 1. Unless we decide the kind of literature we are dealing with, we cannot execute good exegesis. If it is historical prose that is one thing. If it is poetry and myth or saga or symphony that is quite another.

In an unpublished paper delivered to the Rock Symposium, a subcommittee of The Missouri Synod's Committee on Scholarly Research, Robert Preus, of Concordia Seminary, St. Louis, Missouri, has indicated that roughly speaking all interpretations of Genesis fall into two general classifications. First of all, there is approach A. "This approach makes the account figurative, a-historical or supra-historical, and ultimately non-descriptive. The genre of the story will be called myth, poem, parable, epic, saga, depending upon the predilection of the exegete" (Robert Preus, *Different Modern Approaches to the Creation Account of Genesis 1-2*, Thus, the account will be taken as:

1. A demythologized poem sung to the glory of the creator God;
2. An aetiological saga, offering an explanation of questions which must have puzzled the Israelites in the tenth century;
3. A cosmology, like many other epic and legendary cosmologies of the day, but purified of theogony, theomachy, and other unworthy elements;

4. "Inspired" Hebrew borrowing from the sacred writings and legends of near neighbor cultures;
5. A similar reworking of ancient Hebrew myths into one organic account, didactic ,in nature.

These approaches vary considerably. They are alike, however, in having a strong emphasis upon the long development of the creation story and a general eliminating of the possibility that Moses received a divine revelation of what really did take place at creation. They also stress the polemical nature of the account, namely that it is against polytheism and false cosmologies. Parenthetically, the essayist would add at this point that there certainly is a polemical note in Genesis 1. However, these various approaches go on to discount the idea that the Genesis account could possibly be descriptive of what actually happened. Generally, they would say we do not know what happened. We would next note that these are usually tied together very intimately with the documentary hypothesis, and assert that there are divergent accounts on creation in the Old Testament. It is commonly claimed that in Genesis 1 and 2 these divergent theories are allowed to stand side by side with their conflicts unresolved.

Preus points out that there is another approach, namely approach B. "This approach accepts Genesis 1 as a chronological account of something that actually happened in creation. Genesis 1 and 2 offer us correct and satisfactory *information* concerning prehistoric times and urgeschichte." Leupold in his *Exposition of Genesis* (p. 25 ff.) states that the account "goes back beyond the reach of available historical sources and offers not mythical suppositions, not poetical fancies, not vague suggestions, but a positive record of things as they actually transpired and, at the same time, of matters of infinite moment for all mankind."

Preus goes on to say that such an understanding of Genesis 1 and 2 is basic to a full understanding of our doctrine of sin and redemption (law and gospel). "This interpretation insists that the biblical account is utterly superior to the other cosmogonies of the day, and is therefore not a derivative of any of them, although Moses may have been aware of these accounts and used aspects of them. Such an approach in no way implies that metaphors, anthropomorphisms and other figures of speech are not employed, e.g., God speaks, walks in the garden. . . . But in none of these cases may we say that God did nothing. For instance, when God spoke, something happened; this means he did speak."

Preus goes on to indicate that position B has basic theological concerns. "It insists that the Genesis account agree with the rest of Scripture on the themes mentioned (e.g., Romans 5). Thus, theologically, one must insist upon a created universe with a transcendent God (against all forms of pantheism and naturalism), a created human man and woman (against evolutionism and polygenesis), a man created in a state of perfection, and an actual, historical fall (against all mythological explanations of man's present sinful condition). This is interpreting Genesis 1 and 2 in terms of law and gospel."

Still further complicating the picture is the insistence of many interpreters, including some who assert that they hold to verbal inspiration, that Genesis 2 actually contains a separate and conflicting report from Genesis 1. It is said that Genesis 1 represents the writing of the priestly writer who uses the word "Elohim" for God, whereas Genesis 2:4b through 2:24 is an account of the writer designated as J, who used the word "Yahweh" or Jehovah. This immediately plunges us in a consideration of the documentary hypothesis with all of the ramifications thereof. For the purposes of this chapter, I am assuming that there is no conflict in Scripture and that we do not have conflicting elements standing side by side. I am also assuming the correctness of scholars such as Walter A. Maier and George V. Schick, both of them holding doctorates in Hebrew, who rejected the documentary hypothesis. They are not alone in that, however. In a recent publication from Hebrew University in Jerusalem, M. H. Segal says, "The preceding pages have made it clear why we must reject the documentary theory as an explanation of the composition of the Pentateuch. The theory is complicated, artificial and anomolous. It is based upon unproved assumptions. It uses unreliable criteria for the separation of the text into component documents." (*Scripta Hirosolymitana*, vol. 8, "Studies in the Bible," editor Chaim Robin, Jerusalem: Moques Press, Hebrew University, 1961, p. 95).

Segal goes on to examine the alleged duplications of several accounts which are to be found in Genesis, and he says as follows, "A careful examination of these narratives will show that the alleged duplication is either only apparent or is based upon an incorrect exegesis. Thus it is said that Genesis 2:4 gives another story of the creation belonging to the J document as distinguished from the preceding story in Genesis 1:2-3 which is assigned to the P document. But 2:4 cannot be like 1:1—2:3, an account of the creation of the world, since it says nothing of the creation of the firmament, the seas, the luminaries and other essential elements of the world. The truth is that 2:4 and following is an integral part of the story of man's sin and punishment.

Its purpose is to describe the environment of man before his sin, the garden and its plants and its animals, and the detailed creation of the woman. The description differs indeed in its style and viewpoint and in some details from the story in 1:1–2:3, but it is not sufficient to prove a different author." This is in harmony with the traditional position that in Genesis 2 we have a zooming in of the lens of revelation to tell us what happened in the Garden of Eden as distinct from the events at large in the universe and the planet earth.

Are Genesis Chapters 1 and 2 Historical?

But this still leaves unanswered the question as to whether or not the accounts in Genesis 1 and 2 are in fact historical. In support of taking the Genesis 1 and 2 account as a recording of what did in fact take place we note the following supporting evidence.

First, the form as we have it is essentially a straightforward prose account. While it contains certain lofty concepts and figures of speech such as anthropomorphisms, there is no indication that it is anything but a factual account. We do not think of it as history in the sense that it is verifiable history, as for example the history of the Civil War where one may go back and do research in terms of establishing a certain point of interest. It is history which must have been based on revelation, but history nonetheless in the sense that it is an account of what actually did happen. It is interesting that the Jewish scholar, E. A. Speiser, in his commentary in the Anchor Bible translation of Genesis, appears to support this assertion. He says, "What we have here is not primarily a description of events or a reflection of a unique experience. Rather we are given the barest statement of a sequence of facts resulting from the fiat of supreme and absolute master of the universe . . . the ultimate objective was to set forth in a manner that must not presume in any way to edit the achievement of the creator — by the slightest injection of sentiment or personality — not a theory, but a credo untinged by the least hint of speculation, Genesis 1 through 11 in general and the first section in particular are a broad introduction to the *history* which commences with Abraham. The practice of tracing history back to antediluvian times is at least as old as the Sumerian king list" (E. A. Speiser, "The Anchor Bible," *Genesis*, Garden City, New York: Doubleday and Co., 1964, pp. 8-9).

The concept that Genesis is indeed historical is supported by the genealogical list in Genesis 5 where we are told of the birth of Seth who in turn was the father of Enoch, who was the father of Cainan, etc., until we come to Noah. The same list occurs in Luke 3 and one cannot avoid the conclusion that there is a reference here to real people. Certainly there is no parallel for this kind of procedure in the poetic literature of the Old Testament.

Another consideration is the phrase in Luke 2:4: "These are the generations of the heavens and the earth when they were created." This same formula is found in Genesis 5:1 where it says this is the "record of the line" of Adam, 6:9 where it is translated this is the "line" of Noah, 10:1 where it is translated these are the "lines" of Noah's three sons, and in Genesis 11:10, 11:27, 25:12, 25:19, 36:1, 36:9, 37:2. Oesch points out that this formula stands as a superscription over a historical listing which is to follow. Since it stands over the account of Adam and the special creation of Eve in the same manner that it stands over other historical listings, it would point to Genesis 2 as being historically factual. Some commentators try to evade this by saying that the passage cannot be a superscription, but must be a subscription of what went before. This would still actually indicate that it was a factual account, but is rejected by Oesch. He points out that this is the beginning of a narrative, the main address. After the statement in Genesis 2:1, that the heavens and the earth were finished and that God had finished his work, the author goes on to tell the story of mankind in its relationship to God and to focus on the story of the fall (Oesch, *op. cit.*).

Against these indications of the historical nature of Genesis 1 and 2, several approaches have been set forth in the interest of viewing Genesis 1 and 2 as accounts which are polemical against heathen concepts and which teach the sovereignty to God, the goodness of God, etc., but which teach nothing concerning the so-called "how of creation." It has been said that the chief purpose of Genesis is to serve as praise and that it is one of several portraits of creation given in the Bible. Other portraits are Psalm 104, Proverbs 8, and Job 38 and 39. The implication is that all of these accounts are ways in which the Jews praised God the creator. The basic weakness of this approach lies in the presupposition that because there are psalms of praise to the creator in the Bible, the Genesis account must by virtue of that very fact be one of these. It really begs the question by asserting what is to be proved. An examination of Psalm 104 and a comparison of this Psalm with the Genesis 1 and 2 account makes clear the vast difference that is there. First of all, the Psalm account has the characteristic Hebrew parallelism of phrases and sentences which is the form of Hebrew poetry. Genesis does not have this.

Furthermore, Psalm 104 starts out with the words, "Bless the Lord, O my soul! O Lord my God, Thou art very great. . . ." It thus clearly indicates that it is a hymn of blessing. This is quite different from the beginning of Genesis which says, "In the beginning God created." One labels itself as a hymn of praise, the other says nothing about it.

Furthermore, it is incorrect to label accounts such as Psalm 104 as creation accounts. Psalm 104 makes no reference to the creation of animals and no reference to the creation of man. Another account which is sometimes mentioned is Proverbs 8. Here is no mention made of sun, moon and stars or of animals or of man or of woman. These same arguments apply to Job 38, 39. These are undoubtedly references to the creation account. But they are built on the supposition that everyone knows the account of Genesis 1 and 2 and these are reflections on various phases of the creative activity. This in no way indicates that the Genesis account is of the same nature as the poetic reflections thereon. It is much the same fallacy as to say that Genesis 1 and 2 cannot be factual because the last book in the Bible is Revelation and this is apocalyptic in nature. There is no logical or theological basis for assertions of this kind.

More to the point is the endeavor of those individuals who point out that there are certain figurative expressions in Genesis. Reference is made to the fact that God is described as speaking, that he breathes into man's nostrils, that he molds man from the dust of the earth, etc. The argumentation is that these anthropomorphic elements lead us to believe that we are dealing with an extended figurative expression.

An examination of the use of anthropomorphisms in the Bible leads to the conclusion that their presence in an account does not "ipso facto" render the account a figurative or poetic account. For example, in Genesis 11:29 we read, "It came to pass when God destroyed the city of the plain that God *remembered* Abraham." The fact that the anthropomorphic expression "remembered" is used does not take away from the historical account that the cities were actually destroyed. In Exodus 3:8, God says, "I am *come down* to deliver them out of the hand of the Egyptians." Again the fact that God is spoken of as coming down does not mean that there was no deliverance out of the bondage in Egypt. Similarly Christ in Luke 11:20 says, "By the finger of God I cast out demons." The reference to the finger of God would certainly not mean that the casting out of the demons is something which did not actually take place. We would conclude that it takes something more than the presence of an anthropomorphism to render an account non-prose and non-factual.

Young also points out that while there are anthropomorphic terms in Genesis 2, they are rather limited. He adds, "the words 'and God breathes' may be termed anthropomorphic, but that is the extent to which the term is employed. The man was real, the dust was real, the ground was real, as was also the breath of life. To these elements of the verse the term anthropomorphism cannot be legitimately applied" (*op. cit.*).

Another point is made that the numbers 7 and 10 occur rather strikingly in the Genesis account and that the activity of the first three days respectively can be connected with the activity of the last three days respectively. For example, on the first day light was created and on the corresponding fourth day of the second triad, the heavenly bodies were placed in the sky. It is argued that this formal relationship indicates a type of literature which is structured so as to present a story which might easily be memorized. It is concluded because of this that the events recorded are not chronologically narrated or even correspond in any way specifically to what may or may not have happened.

In reply we would note the following. The fact that there may be a formal structured system in the account may not indicate at all that the account is artificial. It may merely point to an orderly procedure on the part of God. Frederick A. Filby, professor of physics at the University of London, points out that there is mathematical pattern in nature itself. He mentions the structures of molecules, the lattices of chemical crystals, the arrangement of leaves on the stems of trees, etc. And then he adds, "It is but one step further to realize that the mathematical mind that designed the universe has revealed itself through the pattern of works in Genesis 1" (*Op. cit.*, p. 19).

The same answer might be given to those who say that the reason for the seven days of creation is to explain why the Jews had to rest on the sabbath day. This approach assumes that the story is written to justify the law rather than that the law reflects the actual order of creation. It is significant that the six periods of activity occur rather commonly in many of the creation myths of other peoples. It seems to point back to a very early establishment of six as a significant number. The late Professor G. C. Aalders of the Free University of Amsterdam has said, "Exodus 20, verse 11, speaks of the activity of God which man is to follow. How could man be held accountable for working six days if God himself had not actually worked for six days? (Edward J. Young, *Westminster Theological Journal*, Nov., 1962, p. 5).

Concerning the scheme of the first three days forming a triad which corresponds to the last three days which form a corresponding triad with day 1 corresponding to day 4, day 2 to day 5 and day 3 to day 6, it may be observed that this scheme does not hold up on thorough analysis. For example, the light bearers are placed in the firmament on day 4. Day 4 is supposed to correspond to day 1 on which light is created. That is all right. However, they are placed in the firmament on day 4, but the firmament was not made until day 2 and actually should correspond to activities on day 5. Thus the parallelism is imperfect in that day 4 refers to things made on both day 1 and day 2. Another example is the fact that the fish were commanded to swim in the seas on day 5, but the seas were not made until the third day which corresponds in the supposed scheme of parallelism to the sixth day instead of the fifth day. There are other points in the account which indicate the same lack of parallelism. These points are thoroughly explored by Dr. Young in the articles in the *Westminster Theological Journal* to which we previously referred.

In other words, while there is a certain general framework it is not a stilted form of artificial framework which might lead us to believe that the events were arranged in a non-chronological order. Moreover, it is to be noted that even within the framework hypothesis there is preserved a certain amount of chronology because the events follow in terms of day 1, 2 and 3 and days 4, 5, and 6.

It might be further noted that the arrangement of items in a specific framework does not thereby invalidate these being references to actual facts. A classic example is the genealogy of Christ in the Gospel of Matthew, tracing Christ back to Abraham. The genealogy is arranged into fourteen generations from Abraham to David, fourteen from David to the deportation to Babylon and fourteen from the deportation to Babylon to Christ. The framework is such that the actual genealogy as found in I Chronicles is abridged by the omission of four names so as to fit the fourteen-fourteen-fourteen scheme. Nonetheless it serves the purpose of showing that Christ was a descendant of Abraham according to his legal genealogy which is given here. No one would say that the framework which is used here means that the individuals in the list were not real individuals. The existence of some framework does not justify us in concluding that the events which are recorded may not be factual events. I understand that some scholars also claim that John's Gospel is arranged on the basis of seven days.

Thus it would appear that the position that the account in Genesis 1 and 2 is historical in the sense of providing prehistory and referring to actual events may still be maintained. There is no compelling reason in Scripture for deviating from what is the manifestly first impression one reaches when he examines the text.

A Closer Look

Let us go on to an examination of specific words and phrases in Genesis 1 and 2 to see if they lend themselves to theistic evolution. It has been held that the expression in Genesis 1:11, "Let the earth put forth vegetation, plants yielding seed and fruit trees" and the expression in verse 20, "Let the waters bring forth swarms of living creatures and let birds fly above the earth across the firmament of the heavens" is indicative of evolution. It is said to refer to a process of development rather than to a fiat creation in response to God's word. However, if Moses were describing an evolutionary process, one would expect it to have been phrased differently, that out of the earth and seas came a simpler form of life, which in turn produced a higher form of life. It is probably best to conclude as does Norman Habel in a series of unpublished theses that "No hidden clue of evolution can be legitimately extracted from this passage." It is more likely that what is discussed here is the fact that once these things sprang forth in response to God's creative word, the process of God's providence took over. This is parallel to man being told to fill the earth and subdue a process which certainly would involve a period of time.

One could also mention that the birds are pretty well left high and dry if this was an evolutionary process, because although the ground is to bear the vegetation and the waters the swarms of living creatures, the birds are simply "to fly" with no reference to any source for them. This would fit response to a creative word, but not an evolutionary process.

Chapter 2 of Genesis has several points in it which are incompatible with human evolution. First of all there is the creation of Adam. We are told that, "The Lord God formed man of dust from the ground and breathed into his nostrils the breath of life and man became a living being." If evolution were true, and if Genesis in any way reflects anything that actually did take place, then one would not expect man to be derived from dust but rather from living material. It is worth mentioning that the word translated as dust in the Revised Standard Version is "apar" in the Hebrew. In the Anchor Bible it is described as standing for "lumps of earth, soil, dirt" as well as the resulting particles of dust. The new version translates "God Yahweh formed man from clods of soil" which to the Jew certainly represented non-living material. Any hint of origin from living organisms is ruled out by the phrase "man became a living being." In a paper prepared for the Proviso Pastor and Teachers Conference in February of 1962, Paul Bretcher has the following paragraph. "Man is a distinctive creation; Genesis 1:21 states that God created every living creature (nephesh hayah) which the waters brought forth, and verse 24 states 'That God said let the earth bring forth the living creature (nephesh hayah) . . . of the earth.' Then Genesis 2:7 states, 'And the Lord God formed man . . . and man became a living soul' (nephesh hayah) presumably for the first time. So it would certainly seem from this that man was not derived from any pre-existing line of 'nephesh' or living creatures."

It is significant also that Genesis 2:20 records that man surveyed cattle and birds and beasts of the field, but that "for the man there was not found a helper fit for him." Regardless of the literary form of the Genesis account, the message here is loud and clear. Man, Adam, is distinct from all the animals which he surveyed, and there was no one like him. This is a completely impossible concept under the theory of evolution where Adam would have been one of several anthropoid hominids who were approaching the status of homo, through a series of mutations. There would have been many other pre-men and women like him or at least a number of them. Certainly he would not have surveyed all of the animal kingdom and found no one who would be a helpmeet for him.

This is emphasized by the creation of Eve which follows where she is taken from man and recognized as being "at last bone of my bones and flesh of my flesh" (Genesis 2:23). The whole emphasis on sex at this point would again be pure nonsense if theistic evolution were involved, because sex would have originated many, many millions of years previous to this.

It is interesting how some Catholic biologists who attempt to keep the reality of Adam and Eve and who want to accomodate themselves to evolution wrestle with the problem of the origin of Eve. P. G. Fothergill, in his book *Evolution and Christians*, proposes a number of explanations. One is that Adam was "the product of pre-hominid parents acting as instrumental causes." He goes on to say that Adam then would have married one of the near-human creatures which he lived with. He would have then produced a child which would have been "the product of a fully-formed human male gamete and a near-human female egg. As a single gamete itself contains all of the potentialities of the offspring, the child would have been human in the true and full sense of the term, and could have received a human soul in the way we all do. It would have been formed from the body of Adam in the most natural and intimate way. Such a child could have been Eve." He goes on to indicate that Adam then married Eve, and thus Eve could be truly spoken of as having been out of Adam (*Evolution and Christians*, London: Longmans, 1961, p. 327). I leave it to you to decide how satisfactory such an explanation might be.

Sin and Death

Unless Genesis 1, 2, and 3 are taken as historical and practical, there is no satisfactory explanation of the origin of sin and death. The continual emphasis upon the goodness of creation and man's being created in the image of God does not fit an evolutionary scene. For sin and death and destruction, the law of tooth and fang, the survival of the fittest, would have been a commonplace part of the world from the very beginning. So would have been death. Genesis tells us and is supported by the New Testament that sin and death originated through the fall of Adam and Eve. In this connection Alexander Heidel's opinion is worth quoting (*Gilgamesh Epic and Old Testament Parallels*, 1949, pp. 142-3), "The presence of the tree of life in the garden of Eden shows that man was intended from the beginning to live forever. Through sin he forfeited this privilege and at the very moment of his transgression entered upon the road of death. Man's state before the fall was not one of absolute immortality, or of absolute freedom from death, in which sense God and the angels are immortal, but rather one of relative or conditional immortality. This could have been turned into absolute immortality by man's eating of the tree of life, which had the power, naturally bestowed upon it by its creator (2:9) to impart imperishable physical life (3:22). But from this he was prevented after the fall by being banished from the garden, since the acquisition of imperishability by sinful man would have entailed his continuance in sin forever and would have precluded the possibility of his renewal or restoration. Contrary to F. Schwally, Genesis 3:19 does not attribute the cause of death to the original composition of the human body, so that man would ultimately have died anyway, but states merely one of the consequences of death: since the human body was formed from the dust of the earth, it shall, upon death, be resolved to earth again. Nowhere in the

Old Testament is death regarded as a part of man's God-given constitution, or as the natural end of life. Nor is it indicated anywhere that death already existed before sin, but became a punishment through sin."

It is highly interesting that theistic evolutionists are unable to give a satisfactory explanation for this origin of death. Helmut Thielicke, for example, says, "This is the dramatic part in our story — it is this: that this arrogant man who wanted no limitations put upon him, this man who wanted to snatch God's eternity for himself, who wanted to be immortal and like God, has his limitations cast into his teeth. 'The man has become like one of us,' the story says, 'knowing good and evil.' After he has nibbled at the tree of knowledge, he will also reach out for the tree of life and plunder the fruit of immortality. He will want to be unlimited in time, he will want to be eternal. Therefore he is driven out of Paradise, and the burden of mortality is placed upon his back. In other words, *the unlimited one is shown his limits*" (*How the World Began,* Philadelphia: Muhlenberg Press, 1961, pp. 174-6) In other words, Thielicke claims that man was originally mortal and that his sin merely was that he aspired to be immortal in an arrogant attitude. As a consequence, his pre-existent mortality is flung in his face.

Gerhard von Rad in his commentary deals with this question of death as a problem where he speaks of the various difficulties. In an attempt to explain it from the viewpoint of man already being mortal since his origin was in dust, he stumbles over the fact that then God's threat "you will die" is really meaningless since God did not follow out the threat at that time and extended his grace and permitted him to die later. Since he was to die later anyway, God obviously did not keep his word. He also regards as exegetically embarrassing the reference to the tree of life. Why was this in the garden if man was mortal originally and supposed to return to the dust and actually had been returning to the dust all along in terms of his ancestors. He speaks of this as a fresh difficulty and says, "Could man after all, after a sentencing, break through the ban of death?" (Gerhard von Rad, *Genesis,* Philadelphia: Westminster Press, 1961, pp. 92-3)

Eden

It is sometimes claimed that the description of the garden of Eden is proof of the lack of historicity of Genesis 2. It is pointed out that in addition to the river Hiddekel which is the Sumerian term for the Tigres River and the reference to the Euphrates, both of which are in Mesopotamia, there is a reference to the river Pishon and Gihon. Gihon is said to be flowing about the whole land of Kush and Pishon is said to flow around the land of Havilah. It is also pointed out that Genesis 2:10 indicates that it was one river that flowed out of Eden and became four rivers. It is said that since the Gihon was evidently the Nile and that the Pishon perhaps may have been the Ganges or Indus River, the geography is impossible. This is said to show that the author really wasn't concerned with giving a historical account. In this connection it is interesting to read what E. A. Speiser says in the Anchor Bible commentary on Genesis. He states, "Recent data on the subject (of the location of Eden) demonstrates that the physical background of the tale is authentic. All four streams once converged or were believed to have done so, near the head of the Persian Gulf, to create a rich garden land to which religion and literature alike look back as the land of the blessed. And while the Pishon and Gihon stand for lesser streams, which have been Hebraized into something like 'the gusher' and 'the bubbler' respectively, the Tigres and the Euphrates leave no doubt in any case as to the assumed locale of the garden of Eden. The chaotic geography of ancient and modern exponents of this biblical text can be traced largely to two factors. One is the mistaken identification of the land of Kush in verse 13 with the homonymous biblical term for Ethiopia rather than with the country of the Kassites; note the spelling 'kussu' in the Nuzi document and the classical Greek form 'kossaios.' The other adverse factor is linked with specialized Hebrew usage. In verse 10 the term 'head' can have nothing to do with streams into which the river breaks up after it leaves Eden, but designates instead four separate branches which have merged within Eden. There is thus no basis for detouring the Gihon to Ethiopia, not to mention the search for the Pishon in various remote regions of the world" (op. cit., pp. 19-20). It would thus appear that more recent studies have indicated that perhaps the location of the garden of Eden is not so impossible historically after all.

Does the New Testament Shed Light on This Question?

As Christians, we embrace the hermeneutical principle that the Scripture is the best interpreter of Scripture and that the New Testament casts light upon the Old. When we apply this to some of these troublesome questions in Genesis we do not receive any help in connection with the days which are mentioned in the New Testament once (Heb. 4:4). However, we do receive considerable emphasis upon Adam and Eve, their origin and their experience in the garden, together with the connection this has with the redemptive work of Jesus Christ.

When Peter and John are released from imprisonment, the prayer of the church is to "the sovereign Lord who didst make the heaven and the earth and the sea and everything in them" (Acts 4:24). Paul preaches to the Athenians about "the God who made the world and everything in it, being Lord of heaven and earth." He also speaks of God having "made from one every nation of men who live on all the face of the earth" (Acts 17:24-26). Paul in Romans 8:19 ff., speaks of a creation "subjected to futility" which waits with eager longing for the revealing of the sons of God, for a creation which has "been groaning in travail." In II Corinthians 4:6, Paul talks about the power of the Gospel and says, "It is the God who said, 'Let light shine out of darkness,' who has shone in our hearts to give the light of the knowledge of the glory of God in the face of Christ." In Matthew 19:4 Jesus discusses divorce with the Pharisees and replies, "Have you not read that he who made them from the beginning made them male and female and said for this reason a man shall leave his father and mother and be joined to his wife and the two shall become one so they are no longer two but one?" In verse 8, in reply to the claim of the Pharisees that Moses allowed divorce, he says from the beginning it was not so (Matthew 19:4-9). This, of course, is a direct reference to the institution of marriage as found in Genesis 2.

More specifically regarding Adam and Eve, Paul takes literally the story of the origin of Eve. This is manifest from the reference in I Corinthians 11:8 where he says, "For man was not made from woman but woman from man, neither was man created for woman but woman for man." And in verse 12 where he says, "For as woman was made for man, so man is now born of woman." In I Timothy 2:13, Paul writes, "For Adam was formed first and then Eve and Adam was not deceived but the woman was deceived and became a transgressor." Term formed is *eplasthe* from *plasso*, a word which means to form or mold. The word translated first is *protos* which Lenske points out is a predicate adjective. He comments, "Adam was created as the first. He existed for some time before Eve was formed." The same position is taken by the Arndt-Gingrich Lexicon. It states "Protos" is used "as a predicate adjective when an adverb can be used in English." It is translated "as the first one." I Timothy 2:13 is cited as one example of this usage (Wm. F. Arndt and F. Wilbur Gingrich,

Greek-English Lexicon of the New Testament, University of Chicago Press, 1957, pp. 732-3).

More central is the reference to Adam and his sin as we find it in Romans 5 where Adam is contrasted with Christ. In verse 12 it reads, "Therefore as sin came into the world through one man and death through sin, and so death spread to all men because all men sinned." In verse 17 it reads, "If because of one man's trespass, death reigned through that one man, much more will those who receive the abundance of grace and the free gift of righteousness reign in life through the one man Jesus Christ. Then as one man's trespass led to condemnation for all men, so one man's act of righteousness leads to acquittal and life for all men." In a recent article in the *Concordia Theological Monthly,* Walter R. Roehrs, a Lutheran Hebrew scholar, points out that this passage as well as the reference in I Corinthians leaves no doubt as to the actuality of the fall of Adam and Eve as two individuals who fell from a perfect state and plunged mankind into sin. He says, "Scripture clearly derives the need of all men for a restoration to the primeval relationship to God from the fall of the first parents of man. The actuality of the fall of Adam and Eve, two individuals, is the unargued presupposition for the lost condition of all men and of the necessity of a Savior from sin. The insistence that there is only one Savior is predicated on the fact that there was only one through whom the need of redemption rose. This is the point that is made in I Corinthians 15:44-49, 57, as well as in Romans 5:12, 15-19 (cf. also I Timothy 2:13-14; I Corinthians 11:8-9)" "The Creation Account of Genesis," May, 1965, pp. 317-318).

Anyone who is acquainted with the theory of evolution knows that it is impossible to reconcile with any theory of evolution a historic Adam and Eve who are sinless creatures created in the image of God, not subject to death, and the parents of all mankind. The theory of evolution has no place for the image of God. Man is a brute and arises gradually from a brute ancestry. Death is present at the very beginning. There would have been an evolutionary population, not a single couple such as Adam and Eve. We would conclude then that the concept of theistic evolution is incompatible with the New Testament passages on creation and the fall of man.

The Philosophical Platform

One might then go on to ask, Is the theory of theistic evolution compatible philosophically with Christianity?

Before going into this, it is worthwhile to note that the hope for reconciliation of tension between the theory of evolution and Christianity as a supernatural religion is not eliminated by the compromise of saying that evolution is God's way of creating. If you say that, you then inject into the scientific theory of evolution a supernatural factor. Robert Preus, in a personal note, indicates, "It occurs to me that the position of the theistic evolutionist (on scientific grounds) is more precarious than that of the creationists. The creationist has in effect made the great step which I just spoke of. He has denied to the scientist (qua scientist) to operate without consideration of divine creation and intervention into nature (an utterly audacious position to take today). At the same time he would insist that the very verification principle used by the scientists is quite theoretically possible of application to such phenomena as miracles and creation itself, e.g., cf. the authentic records of miracles and the revelation of God in nature. This implies that theology qualifies as knowledge just as science and is gained empirically. Revelation is a historical datum capable of yielding knowledge. The theistic evolutionist seems thus to be neither fowl nor fish. He cannot claim to be consistent with the principles of modern science, for the reasons listed above, nor of theology."

This is precisely the point made by George Gaylord Simpson in a recent book. He examines the so-called attempt to inject vitalism or mysticism (his words for the supernatural guidance of God of the process) on the part of three famous men: LeCompte DuNouy, Edmund W. Sinnott, and Theilhard De Chardin. He concludes, "Three great men and great souls, and all have flatly failed in their quest. It is unlikely that others can succeed where they did not, and surely I know of none who has. The attempt to build an evolutionary theory mingling mysticism and science has only tended to vitiate the science. I strongly suspect that it has been equally damaging on the religious side, but here I am less qualified to judge" (*This View of Life*, New York: Harcourt Brace Co., 1964, p. 232). Precisely the same point is made by Curtly F. Mather of Harvard University in a recent publication. He states, "When a theologian accepts evolution as the process used by the creator, he must be willing to go all the way with it. Not only is it an orderly process, it is a continuing one. Nothing was finished on any seventh day; the process of creation is still going on. The golden age for man — if any — is in the future, not in the past . . . Moreover the creative process of evolution is not to be interrupted by any supernatural intervention . . . the spiritual aspects of the life of man are just as surely a product of the processes called evolution as are his brain and nervous system" (*Science Ponders Religion*, edited by Harlow Shapley, New York: Appleton Century Croft, Inc., 1960, pp. 37-38).

Thus it would appear that if we sacrifice our interpretation of Genesis to naturalism, we are then called upon to go all the way. As a matter of fact a number of evolutionists have been quite clear in the implications which they draw from the process. Julian Huxley has stated, "God is unnecessary" (*Time*, August 1, 1960, p. 45). G. G. Simpson has referred to Christianity as a higher form of superstition which in some ways is actually inferior to the superstitions of the native tribes. He has referred to church services as "higher superstitions celebrated weekly in every hamlet of the United States" (*Science*, April 1, 1960, p. 966). In other words, once the premise of evolution is granted that matter interacts with itself and under the guidance of the process of natural selection, there is no need of God. Theistic evolutionists, of course, would deny this. In effect they would attempt to baptize the theory and to make it Christian. After two decades of reading evolutionary literature, both philosophical and scientific, I am of the opinion that this baptizing cannot be effected. The theory is based on the interaction of matter with matter. It is based on the changes which are produced by chance and which are then developed by natural selection. If one places God's guidance into the process he violates one of the basic tenets of the theory. Moreover, evolution has no place for a man starting in a good world, a man starting with a knowledge of righteousness and true holiness (Ephesians 4:24; Colossians 3:10). Man does not fall from a lofty position. Rather he is climbing upward under his own power from a lower position achieving a higher one. This is the basic rationale of evolution and cannot be separated from it.

That this is not my personal bias can be demonstrated by several sources. There is a recent work by Paul Raubiczak, a professor of philosophy at Cambridge University. The title of the book is *Existentialism — For and Against* (Cambridge University Press, 1964). In this book Raubiczak points out that the theories of Darwinism and his descendents have many gaps. The theory does not explain the origin of matter. It does not explain the irregularity in matter which is necessary for certain of the cosmological theories from the viewpoint of its origin. It does not explain the origin of purpose. It does not explain the origin of life and the different quality of human mind. He then states, "The theory of evolution shows, as do all theories, the limitations of knowledge. It should not therefore be accepted as a complete basis for philosophy, or as ultimate absolute truth. Scientists are fully entitled to make it the basis of research, but philosophers should consider its limitations critically" (p. 23).

Raubiczak then goes on to say, "Nevertheless evolution has been made the basis of a complete philosophy. It provided philosophers with a metaphysical and ethical system, thus deeply influencing their ideas about the nature of man and his behavior. In fact the philosophy based on Darwinism has exercised an extremely strong influence, far beyond the realms of science and philosophy upon the whole development of European thought. The ruthless life and death struggle for survival has been translated into a new morality, as ruthless competition in a capitalist, as ruthless warfare in the communist world, and as ruthless nationalism everywhere. Moreover, for the first time in human history, mind and reason are no longer seen as some mysterious higher power, as part of a supernatural, divine sphere breaking in upon human existence, but as the product of lower, biological factors, and nothing has done more to fortify materialism. The word spirit has lost all its meaning, and human mind itself has been impoverished" (ibid.).

Raubiczak goes on to discuss Nietzsche. He asserts that Nietzsche in his philosophy is dependent upon Darwinism and its philosophy. He says, "His next step fits in, once more with the demands of philosophical Darwinism: God has to be dismissed as well. He emphasizes again and again, 'God is dead,' and asks rhetorically, 'What thinker still needs the hypothesis of God?'" (p. 28). Raubiczak also asserts that Nietzsche's theory of heredity shows the influence of Darwinism and his philosophy. "He continually demands the breeding of a new master race and the prohibition for its sake of the reproduction of all the 'discontented, the rancorous, and the grudging,' the sterilization of criminals and 'the annihilation of millions of misfits.' The spectre of the Nazi gas chambers looms behind such statements . . . we must not forget that it is not only Nietzsche's philosophy, but also the theory of evolution which leads to such consequences (Nazism)" (pp. 35-36).

It is hardly necessary to point out the unChristian and unbiblical nature of the entire tenor of the philosophy of evolution. It is evident from the writings of evolutionists, both in the area of science and in the area of philosophy, that this philosophy can no more be separated from the theory than dye can be separated when a sweater has been permanently dyed any given color. It becomes a part of the very warp and woof of the substance. When an attempt of separation is made the cry of vitalism and supernaturalism is made by the scientists on the one hand. On the other hand it is evident theologically that basic doctrines such as the nature of man, the origin of death, original sin, etc., are placed in jeopardy if not denied completely.

Conclusion

It would seem better to accept in simple faith the account of the origin of man as given in the book of Genesis, to allow scientists to continue to pursue their research, but to insist on what Scripture tells us concerning man's origin and his purpose in life as well as the redemption which God has wrought for us in Jesus Christ. It would be tragic if we were to permit scientific theories, scientific philosophies, to dictate our theology either explicitly or implicitly. Let us really let the Scriptures speak to us and not attempt to read into them many things which even liberal commentaries insist the authors never thought of.

Finally, let us not despair if we cannot find all the answers. As Alan Richardson, the British scholar, has so aptly said, "Christian faith is not 'a religion,' one of the various 'religions' of the world, just as God is not 'a god,' one of the mythological deities who have gone down before the advancing armies of modern knowledge. We need not tremble for the ark of God, who still dwells between the cherubim and still is powerful to save; we stand in mortal peril only if in our presumptious unbelief we stretch out our hand to protect the ark, as though we could defend God (cf. I Samuel 4:3; II Samuel 6:6 ff.). It is not we who must go in quest of God and prove that we know him; it is God who calls His people by their name, though they have not known Him; He is Yahweh, and beside Him there is no god (Isaiah 45:4 ff.)" (*The Bible in the Age of Science*, Philadelphia: Westminster Press, 1961, pp. 150-151).

The Origins of Civilization
by R. Clyde McCone

R. CLYDE McCONE

Dr. McCone is Associate Professor of Anthropology at California State College. Prior to accepting this position, he taught at Michigan State University, and South Dakota State College, and served as pulpit supply or pastor of a number of churches of different denominations in South Dakota and Montana.

Dr. McCone holds a B.A. in Religion from Wessington Springs College, a M.S. in Sociology from South Dakota State College, and a PhD. in Anthropology and Sociology from Michigan State University.

IV

THE ORIGINS OF CIVILIZATION:
The Biblical Record and Problems of Historical Explanation

In the discussion of archeological data and problems of evolutionary interpretation of the origins of civilization, we were confronted with a people called the Sumerians who seemed to stand at the meeting point of history and prehistory. They appeared to be at once the avenue of pushing the boundaries of our historical knowledge of man farther into the past and also a forbidding barrier because of the mythological understanding of their world and of their own past. The sacred writings of the Hebrews have given to us an identification of these people in the expression "land of Shinar." It was to this land that peoples in the east migrated, then took counsel, and eventually built a tower to reach unto heaven only to have God confound their language so that they could not understand each other's speech. According to the account of the Hebrews, there lived some centuries later in what was at that time the capital and center of Sumerian culture, a man called Abram. God called him out of Ur from country and kindred and house so that he would show him and give to him a land, promising to bless him and through him to bless the whole world. These promises were renewed to his son and grandson, Isaac and Jacob. One of Jacob's sons, Joseph, was sold by his brothers into Egypt. He, through a series of miraculous incidents, was made second in rank to Pharaoh. His activities regarding the famine not only preserved Egypt but provided a refuge for his father, Jacob, as well as his brothers and their families. After a stay of some generations in Egypt in which the rulers eventually made them slaves, God undertook through Moses to free them and lead them back to the land of Promise. It is this Moses who not only was used to work miracles of deliverance and give to his people the Ten Commandments from Mt. Sinai, but who also is credited with giving to his people a written record that provided them with a connecting link of events and lives with the Abram who had been called out of Ur of Chaldees. But Moses' Record goes much farther than that. Mainly via the means of geneologies the record continues past Abram to the land of Shinar and the town of Babel, and still farther to a world-destroying flood and the rescue of eight people and a large cargo of animal life in the ark. And still the record reaches into the past till there is given the creation of man and the world and the universe in which he lives.

It would appear that in the Hebrew record we are taken back to the very beginning via historical events rather than over the route of evolutionary assumptions.

However, at this point a protest would be raised by many and that is to remind us that the Sumerians also had myths about a beginning and about a flood and its survivors from whom they had descended. And since Abraham was a Semite who came out of Ur of the Chaldees, the Hebrew myth is to be traced through him to the earlier Sumerian myths.

In response to this mythical designation of the Genesis account, two things need to be said. The second is far more important than the first. First, a brief observation about myths and their connection with actual events. At one time, all myths were thought to be purely fictional presentations of the imagination of man. It was thought they may have been the medium of symbolic or moral teaching truths but nothing more. The Homeric poems were regarded by many in this light. Heinrick Schliemann however "naively" believed that there was some actual event truth in the Greek myths. His position was confirmed when the leads provided by the Greek myths led to the archeological discovery of Troy and later to Mycenae. This established as a fact that though the Greeks had understood and written in a mythological manner, the things about which they wrote were events that had actually taken place in time. If we were to accept in this sense the mythological status of the records of Genesis, they probably would still have greater significance for us than would be granted by those who dismiss them by calling them myths. Still, they would suffer from the same kinds of limitations which characterize the Sumerian myths.

At this point we are brought to the second and more important response to the designation of Genesis as myth. By what consistent conceptualization of myth can this Hebrew book be called a myth? There has been a continuing effort in anthropology to arrive at a usuable consistent definition of the term, myth. Though the Sumerian myths do deal with origins and a flood, it is not this that validates our calling these stories myths. It is rather the manner in which these problems and events are presented and also the function which they play in the social life of the people that warrants their designation as myth.

In the mythological narratives of the Sumerians, natural forces are personified and deified. Thus, the sky is Anu who is the highest authority in the polytheistic hierarchy. Enlil is the storm and is understood as the heavenly power conceived in terms of force. So also the earth is dually personified into male principle or water and female principle or soil and by which the productivity of the earth is easily understood. This kind of envolvement of man, deities, and natural forces presented a problem in their explanation of origins. It is not surprising, however, that with this mythological kind of understanding of the world they would have to explain the origin of the gods also. In fact, the Sumerian myths make no distinction in the origin of society, of the gods, and of the world of nature simply because they are inseparable in their thinking. In the beginnings of the development of modern anthropology, Tylor observed this character of myth saying, "First and foremost among the causes which transfigure into myths the fact of daily experience, is the belief in the animation of all nature rising at its highest pitch to personification" (Bidney 1950: 16). The absence of the mythological characteristic in the Genesis account demands the attention of anyone comparing it with these criteria as well as by comparing it with the content of the myths themselves. After contrasting the world views of the Mesopotamian and Egyptian cultures, Henri Frankfort observes their similarity by saying,

> . . . the two peoples agreed in the fundamental assumptions that the individual is part of society, that society is embedded in nature, and that nature is but a manifestation of the divine (Frankfort and Others 1949:241).
> This doctrine was, in fact, universally accepted by the peoples of the ancient world with the single exception of the Hebrews (*Loc. cit.*).

This difference is not only unmistakable but is demanding of attention since the Hebrews came out of the cultural context of the Mesopotamians and spent several centuries within the geographical boundaries and under the political dominance of the Egyptians. Frankfort calls explicit attention to the difference among the Hebrews stating that Yaweh is not in nature. As creator, He is distinct from both man and nature. And also nature is never understood in terms of the biological or psychological characteristics of man. The non-mythological character of the Hebrews views is expressed by Frankfort, "This conception of God represents so high a degree of abstraction that, in reaching it, the Hebrews seem to have left the realm of mythopoeic thought" (*Ibid.*: 244).

A second manner in which anthropologists have defined myth comes from Malinowski, the Polish born, British Social Anthropologist. Malinowski viewed myth in terms of the function which it played in society. Rather than seeing myths as explaining natural phenomena, he sees them as containing and maintaining the basic beliefs which uphold the social order. The myths of ancient civilization also fit this definition. The origin stories not only produced a pantheon of deified, personified forces of nature but also they are related in a power structure to form a divine state. Each city in Mesopotamia was ruled over by its own god who occupied his place in the polytheistic state. When one city fought against another it was perceived as war in heaven, and when a city came out as dominant over the others it was understood that the gods had granted the Anu and Enlil function to the god of that city and his authority was then recognized and respected. The *ensi* or human ruler of the city was regarded as the servant of the god. In this sense the mythology of both Mesopotamia and of Egypt served as the validating foundation of the state for almost three milleniums and as Frankfort observes, without a single rebellion against it. The social order of the city states was functionally inseparable from the mythical belief which supported them.

Here again the origin account of Israel stands out in stark contrast. First, because their belief system existed prior to and apart from their relatively short experience as a nation-state. Second, because in this short existence the people and frequently their leaders rejected or were in conflict with their system of beliefs. Only their prophets and a very small minority of the people remaining true. Third, this belief system continued on beyond the cessation of Israel as a state or a kingdom. The belief system of the mythology of ancient civilization came to a complete end when the social order which it supported ceased. While each of these points could be greatly expanded, they prove conclusively that the beliefs encompassed in the Genesis account are not mythological in the sense of being produced by a cultural process in the social order and of occupying a functional relationship within it.

Utterly apart from the matter of personal commitment to or rejection of the Genesis account, any objective observation using a consistent set of anthropological defining criteria forbids its categorization as myth.

A minimum attention has been given here to handling some of the most important objections to the historical character of the first book of Moses. This has been necessary in order to address our attention more clearly, and with at least less possibility of being misunderstood as to its claims to historical truth. If the label of myth cannot be applied to these opening chapters of our Bible, does it follow that they then may be regarded as history. Here, as with myth, it is important to state what is meant by the term history; is any account that is not myth history, and conversely, if not history, then myth? The popular connotation usually attached to myth is that it is a fanciful creation of the imagination of man and therefore completely lacking in credibility. Similarly, the connotation associated with history is a reliable account of the actual events of the past. Therefore, if any question is raised of the historical status of the Biblical account, this is immediately taken as questioning the actuality of the events recorded, the reliability of the authors, and hence of inspiration of the book itself. I should like to assure you that I have no question of the inspiration of the Book of Genesis, the reliability of its author, whom I have no reason to believe that it was other than Moses, nor the occurrence of the events described. The problem comes only when history is given an explicit definition. History is a human perspective and understanding of the past. It is always a selection, ordering and interpretation of the events of the past structured in some sense within the framework of man's present social conditions. As such, history is in a dual sense a human product, that is, the events are the events of man and the understanding of the events is also the work of man. History as we know it has its beginnings with Herodotus and other early Greek writers. In the thinking of Ernst Cassieer (1953:219), "what we call historical consciousness is a very late product of human civilization. It is not to be found before the time of the Greek historians. And even the Greek thinkers were able to offer a philosophical analysis of the specific forms of historical thought. Such an analysis did not appear until the eighteenth century. The concept of history first reaches maturity in the work of Vico and Herder." Recently Cyrus Gordon has been pointing out the Semitic contributions to the beginnings of Western civilization in Greece, and there can be no question that much later both the Old and New Testament have had a tremendous influence on the thinking of Western man. However much credit the Greeks owe to their Hebrew and other Semitic predecessors, still we must credit them with the beginnings of the writing of history as we know it.

The position which I wish to state and then explicate its meaning is that Genesis cannot be called history in the strict sense that the idea of history has developed in Western civilization and that if it is called history, it is necessary to make explicit certain qualifications. As I attempt to make clear this position, I think you will understand that rather than calling the Biblical account into question, I am only pointing to its unimpeachability.

1. While history as an understanding of the past is a human product, in the same sense the Bible is not. Men were used as the medium of writing the Scriptures. Though they did not write as mechanical robots, yet they were holy men of God moved by the Holy Spirit.

2. The perspective of history is the perspective of man and the locale of human events which is the earth. The perspective of the Bible is that of God and from above. It is a heavenly perspective even though it is focused upon the events of man upon the earth.

3. History is written from the perspective and in the context of the times and of the social order of its writers. Moses as the author of the Pentateuch, of course, did live during a specific period of time and did live in some kind of structured social situation. Neither is it questioned that culturally, he was confined to the resources of his people and time. However, it must be remembered that Israel had remained culturally distinct from the character of ancient civilization. Even when Israel did drift away from God, their prophets were sufficiently detached from social involvement in these movements that they could proclaim a message uninfluenced by them. It is just such messages that give to us the Biblical record of events. They were detached from their time and situation only in the sense that the New Testament writers to the Hebrews could say of their message, "God, who at sundry times and divers manner spake in times past unto the fathers by the prophets, hath in these last days spoken unto us by his Son." It is this character of the Bible, including the Old Testament and the book of Genesis, that though it was written in the distant past and to a people of the past, it has an up-to-date message for every age and every society.

4. The primary purpose of history is to give to man an understanding of his past. More subtly and subjectively it serves to validate the present social situation in which he lives and moves and has his being. The Bible, on the other hand, claims to be a self-revelation of God to man. Rather than validating his present social situation, it raises serious questions about both his past and his present.

5. The points that we have raised are not to discredit history. Nor in questioning the historical character of the Bible have we in any wise called into question the truthfulness of the events recorded in it. To further observe differences between history and the Bible in general, which, of course, includes the Gene-

sis account, it must be observed that the Bible does not give us some things which are necessary for an historical explanation of the past. History requires that we have some arbitrarily chosen point in time from which we measure time and which provides the temporal structure for the relating of events in time. This is not found in the Bible, but it is the kind of thing which is constructed when the Bible is pressed into the mold of the modern conception of history. This is usually done by either taking the point in time that Western man uses, i.e., the birth of Christ, or attempting to measure back to creation as a point in time. Actually, this is an attempt to make "the date" of creation as the arbitrary anchor point in time for a Biblical historiography — or at least chronology. These kinds of efforts to support the Biblical record by giving to it a character of modern history inadvertantly very seriously call it into question. For once creation is made a point in time or a measure of time of any length, it ceases to be creation in the Biblical sense. Time is an integral factor in man's understanding of an existing created order. Space, time, and matter-energy provide the functional constituents of our understanding of the world of nature. As such, "time" is an integral aspect of that which God created. To say that God created the universe at a point in time or in a certain duration of time, whether it be in terms of days or of geological ages, is to make God a creature of time and creation to be something far less than creation. The folly of these attempts may be seen when one carries out the attempt to date creation by some such date as 4004 B.C., September 17th, at 6:00 P.M. on a Saturday evening.

Chronology in Genesis rather than being anchored to an arbitrary point in time is given only in the successive lives of a geneology. It is interesting to observe also that a certain geneology is chosen, i.e., that which follows Seth to Noah rather than the geneology of the descendants of Cain. In this sense the chronology follows a geneology of witnesses. Our modern kind of historiography would have been anchored to some point in the events of the civilization of Cain and other events would have been selected and recorded according to their significance in the development of this social order. In contrast, Genesis gives to us only the fact of the existence of the civilization of Cain and its ultimate destruction at the flood, relating it only to the geneological line of witnesses. The geneology then continues on through the three sons of Noah but the chronology is attached only to the lineage of Shem, reaching to Abram. In each one of the geneologies a statement is inserted relating it to the significant event at Babel. To the lineage of Japheth is simply added the statement,

"By these were the isles of the Gentiles divided in their lands; every one after his tongue, after their families, in their nations." The lineage of Ham through Cush leads to Nimrod of whom it says that he was a mighty hunter before the Lord and that "the beginning of his kingdom was Babel, Erech Accad Calneh, in the land of Shinar." The geneology of Shem leads to Eber which may be the origin of the name Hebrew. Of one of Eber's sons, Peleg, it is stated, "for in his days was the earth divided." The Biblical account of the confusion of language and the diffusion of peoples here in the land of Shinar or of Sumer is identified with all three geneologies but only for that of the line of Shem is there a chronology. The significance of the event as Biblically recorded is primarily in terms of a line of witnesses rather than in the arbitrary framework of the development of a social order. Its significance is not then historical in the modern sense.

Besides lacking the arbitrary temporal structure of history, there is also a lack of the spacial and social particulars which modern historiography calls for. After stating in the opening verse of Genesis 11 that the earth was of one language and one speech we read, "and it came to pass as they journeyed from the east that they found a plain in the land of Shinar and dwelt there." We are not given any social identification, how many they were, in what year, whether this was a mass migration or whether a gradual continuous migration over ten years time or possibly over a century of time. Nor can one deduce how long they dwelt here before the suggestion to build the city arose, nor who it was who made the suggestion, or anything about the social-cultural situation out of which this decision arose. And yet, it is all of these things that history is about. The fact that the Biblical record lacks these necessary features of secular human history in no wise calls into question the credibility of the events which it describes.

In conclusion it should be remembered that the Bible leaves unrecorded untold number of events in the world of nature and the world of man. Man, through the methods of history and pre-history, may attempt to discover records and interpret them. This is a legitimate concern of history, archeology and anthropology. His search may be limited by the amount of undiscovered data remaining hidden in the earth. He may also restrict his own progress if he chooses erroneous assumptions that mislead him in his search. But, in the light of what has been presented we have to conclude first that events revealed to man in the Genesis account cannot be pressed into the mold of history, nor is it a substitute for history. This is to say that we cannot merely hook secular history on to divine revelation at Genesis 11 and claim thereby that we have solved the problem of bridging the gap between history and prehistory by having produced a continuous history from Adam to modern man. But a second conclusion must also be maintained, that is, the events discoverable to man can never be in conflict with the events revealed to man.

These conclusions lead to a closing question which might be phrased something like this: If the record of Genesis is not history in the same manner that modern man has come to understand the past, can it be related to or contribute to modern man's concern with prehistory and of pushing the horizon of history further back? I believe the Bible presents reliable suggestions for the direction that research should take by pointing to the Sumerians. Archeological, linguistic, or any other kind of cultural and historical research of this people promises to yield fruitful results provided the limitations are remembered which were expressed at the close of the paper on archeological data. This kind of research would not have as its object to prove the historical veracity of the Bible or its truth does not rest on these kinds of foundations. Nevertheless, it may well increase our knowledge of man's past. But still, the question may haunt our minds: Will not the time come when historical research and Biblical revelation will be brought together in a common mutually supporting system of the understanding of past events? To this question I would respond, "Not until that day when man stands redeemed side by side with his Redeemer and from the perspective of eternity views the at once tragic and wonderful events of the human drama of time. Then the history of man and divine revelation will be inseparably molded together even as their authors have been reconciled and made one."

Bibliography

The Bible, King James Version

Bidney, David
    The Concept of Myth and the Problem of Psychocultural Evolution. American Anthropologist 52:16-26, 1950.

Cassirer, Ernest
    Essay on Man. Garden City: Doubleday and Company, 1953.

Frankfort, Henry and Others
    Before Philosophy. Baltimore: Penguin Books, Inc., 1949.

The Noachian Flood and Mountain Uplifts

by Donald W. Patten

DONALD W. PATTEN

Donald W. Patten may be called both a businessman and a scholar. A Montanan by birth and a geographer by training and lifelong interest, he began reading the Bible while in college, and shortly thereafter, he experienced conversion. As a student, he was given pulpit duties in a small, rural, community church in the village of Lolo, Montana.

He received a B.A. in geography from the University of Washington in 1951, and a M.A. in 1962. He is owner of a microfilming business in Seattle, and is also the founder of the Pacific Meridian Publishing Company. *The Biblical Flood and the Ice Epoch*, a book investigating the catastrophic nature of the Deluge from the geographical perspective, is his first major publication.

V

THE NOACHIAN FLOOD AND MOUNTAIN UPLIFTS

Part I. The Cosmology of Job

The Book of Job is perhaps the oldest literary resource which is in our possession. In the Book of Job, one finds, next to the gospels, perhaps the most moving and profound blend of drama, pathos and triumph in all literature. The ethic involving Job, his character, his sufferings and his victory is immense in scope. However great this system of moral and spiritual values this ethic in the Book of Job may be, this chapter will bypass this traditional consideration. Rather, it desires to concentrate on the cosmology in the Book of Job, the earth history and the natural science.

Job lived about twelve generations after the flood, approximately the same era as did Abraham.[1] This was an era when worship motifs were generally, and apparently increasingly being directed toward the sun, the moon and the "hosts of heaven," the planetary deities and the sky-gods rather than to the Creator. To this Job objected, and rather strenuously, Job 31:26-29, as did Abraham in Ur of the Chaldees,[2] which was becoming engulfed in themes astrological, complete with astronomer-priests, ziggurats and nature worship.

In terms of a time perspective, Abraham lived ten generations, and Job lived perhaps eleven or twelve generations after the Flood. By comparison, the writer happens to be the tenth generation of his family living on American soil; his earliest American ancestor was in the first wave of the Puritan migration to Massachusetts Bay in 1629. In a sense, we are about as close to the days of the Massachusetts Commonwealth and Plymouth Rock as was Job to the days of the Flood.

However in another sense, Job was closer to the stories and traditions of the Flood. In those days, life did not fade or burn

---

[1]Christine L. Benagh, *Meditations on the Book of Job*, Houston: St. Thomas Press, 1964, pp. 37, 50. "Many of the names of the men and places which figure in Job's story occur conspicuously among the chronicles of the dukes of Edom. . . ."

[2]William Whiston, *The Genuine Works of Flavius Josephus*, Bridgeport: M. Sherman, 1828,pp.94–95 (Ch. VII, Book I).

out as rapidly as today; greater longevity was normal, and generations overlapped many other generations, thus allowing a closer and more vivid account of the early post-diluvian era than we might expect. Thus while Job lived perhaps eight hundred to nine hundred years after the Flood, he was perhaps closer to the Flood in a cultural sense than we are to the founding of our culture some three hundred years ago.

In making an examination or a review of the cosmology of Job, and of some of the natural science contained in the Book of Job, let us recognize first ourselves and our view of cosmology, and note the characteristics of our age. We must do this in order to be certain not to misinterpret the cosmology of Job, for we may easily project, even subconsciously, our concepts into Job's, and call them Job's concepts.

We have lived in an era, the twentieth century, which has happened to be drenched in atheism, in Darwinism and in uniformitarianism. The modern assumption is (to quote the prophet Peter) "all things continue as they were in the beginning" (II Peter 3:4).

Under this cosmological view of gradualism and uniformitarianism, the ice epoch, the so-called ice age came (whatever the cause) very slowly and later gradually retreated, again very slowly, requiring vast amounts of time. Similarly mountains were supposedly uplifted millimeters per millennium until they attained great heights, from which they were subsequently eroded. Modern thought tosses around millions and tens of millions of years like chaff in the wind; the general assumption is "oceans of time for everything" in earth history. This assumption is termed "uniformitarianism." It affects astronomy; it affects geology; it affects biology; it affects world politics; it affects theology.

But although the modern twentieth century world of ours embraces uniformitarianism as an operating assumption, it need not follow that (a) Job's cosmology was uniformitarian, nor (b) need it follow that Job's observations were uniformitarian. Listen to the speeches in Job concerning astronomy and the cosmology of that era. Let us begin by doubting whether Job was a uniformitarian, and let us ask this question periodically. Was Job a uniformitarian?

One of the key thoughts, a crystallizing thought of this chapter, comes from a phrase tucked away in Job 12:8a, "Speak to the earth, and it shall teach thee." We may be considering quickly-drowned mammoths here, and quickly-frozen mammoths later. We shall be considering petrified forests, complete with petrified worms and worm holes, apparently suddenly inundated and suddenly fossilized.

We may be considering fossil bears twenty feet tall, fossil ostriches as large as giraffes, fossil pigs as large as rhinos, fossil sloths weighing ten thousand pounds. We shall be considering turtles found in the fossil record, which possessed shells some ten and twelve feet in diameter. Turtles today generally require a moderate climate and a marine habitat. Now we cannot say that Nebraska and South Dakota possess these characteristics today, but they possess fossil turtles of these dimensions, and much more in the way of fossil animals.

In one location in Nebraska, some eight thousand animals are found, with their skeletons not intact, but rather dismembered or shredded. Among the animals so found, some 90 per cent are to-day extinct, and about 10 per cent have survived as species. The problem of geologists with these bones is to put the right leg bone with the right thigh bone in order to avoid creating some Rube Goldberg animals, because most of the animals so buried have never been seen by modern men.

"Speak to the earth and it shall teach thee." We can gain many insights from the Bible relative to earth history, particularly in the books of Genesis and Job. But the crust of the earth, this vast cemetery of fossils and strata also speaks compellingly of former catastrophes. We might bear in mind dragon flies in the fossil record with wingspans of thirty inches, and birds with wing-spans of twenty and thirty feet. We may bear in mind the Lewis Overthrust in Glacier Park, near the writer's birthplace, where a range of mountains rolled over, or tumbled over upon each other for a distance of thirty to forty miles. We may con-sider the scallop-like or arcuate pattern of mountain uplifts as they grace the crust of our planet in a great circle pattern, and we may note that a similar pattern of orogenetic uplift occurs on the Moon, our planet's binary partner. "Speak to the earth and it shall teach thee."

Orogenesis, or orogeny, is a term which refers to the process of mountain uplifts, or the folding of the earth's crust. Diastrophism relates to the methods of deformation which have sculptured and engraved our planet in the manner in which we find it. Listen to Job 9, and see if you hear anything that sounds like orogeny or deformation.

Then Job answered and said,

> I know it is so of a truth, but how should man be just with God?
> If He will contend with Him, he cannot answer Him one of a thousand.
> He is wise in heart, and mighty in strength: who hath hardened himself against Him and hath prospered?

Which removeth the mountains, and they know it not: *which overturneth them in His anger.*
[Might this sound like a little orogenesis?]
Which shaketh the earth out of her place,
[Might this conceivably refer to the earth's orbit, or a change there in?]
And the pillars thereof tremble.
[This may be particularly interesting for a planet with an axis.]
[And now, Job's mind seems to turn to thoughts wholly astronomical.]
Which commandeth the sun, and it riseth not; and sealeth up the stars.
Which alone spreadeth out the heavens, and treadeth upon the waves of the sea.
Which maketh Arcturus, Orion and Pleiades and the chambers of the south.
[Might the chambers of the south, from Arabia, be correlated to the majestic band of nocturnal brilliance swaddling the tropical skies in nocturnal brilliance, the Milky Way?]
Which doeth great things past finding out; yea, and wonders without number.

Again our question is presented, "Was Job a uniformitarian or was he something else?"
In Job 12:15, apparently the era of the Flood and the immensity of the watery catastrophe comprise the background.

Behold, he withholdeth the waters, and they dry up; also he sendeth them out, and they overturn the earth.

In Job 22, Eliphaz, the miserable comforter with numerous platitudes, discusses the height of heaven, the circuit of heaven, and the generation "whose foundation was overflown with a flood."

He stretcheth out the north over the empty place and hangeth the earth upon nothing. . . .
He hath compassed the waters with bounds, until the day and night come to an end.
The *pillars of heaven* tremble and are astonished at his reproof.
He divideth the sea with His power. . . . By His spirit He hath garnished the heavens (Job 26:7, 10, 11, 12).
He putteth forth His hand upon the rock, He overturneth the mountains by the roots. . . . He bindeth the floods from overflowing (Job 28:9).
[Might this be related to more thought on orogenesis?]

Abraham, like Job, was faced with cultural trends generally favoring astral pantheism, and adoration or worship of the planetary deities, the sky-gods. Both men realized with determination the necessity of opposing the same. Job describes this type of pantheism as follows:

> If I beheld the sun when it shined, or the moon walking in brightness,
>
> And my heart hath been secretly enticed, or my mouth hath kissed my hand,
>
> This also were an iniquity to be punished by the judge (Job 31: 26-28).

Note the similarity of Abraham who, like Job, was something of a twentieth century non-conformist (I did not say twentieth century A.D.). The following comes from Josephus' account of Abraham in Ur of the Chaldees, and his protest, particularly to worship along lines of astral pantheism.

> He was a person of great sagacity, both for understanding all things and persuading his hearers, and not mistaken in his opinions; for which reason he began to have higher notions of virtue than others had, and he determined to renew and to change the opinion all men happened then to have concerning God, for he was the first that ventured *to publish* this notion, that there was but one God the Creator of the universe; and that as to other gods, if they contributed any thing to the happiness of men, that each of them afforded it only according to his appointment, and not by their own power.
>
> This his opinion was derived from the irregular phenomena that were visible both at land and sea as well as those that happened to the *sun and moon, and all the heavenly* bodies thus:
>
> > "If (said he) . . . and here somehow Josephus seems to be quoting Abraham . . . these bodies had power of their own, they would certainly take care of their own regular motions; but since they do not preserve such regularity, they make it plain that so far as they co-operate to our advantage, they do it not of their own abilities, but as they are subservient to him that commands them, to whom alone we ought justly to offer our honor and thanksgiving."[3]

Where Josephus gets his authority to seemingly quote Abraham, I do not know. However it would appear that the issue involved the Babylonian pantheon, which was later translated into Greek as Apollo, Aphrodite, Ares, Pallas Athene, Electra, Zeus and others. Part of the issue, to Abraham, concerned whether or not the

---

[3]Whiston, *loc. cit.*

planets merited worship. But another part of the issue revolved around regular versus irregular motions in the heavens, or predictable versus unpredictable movements.

This was an issue for Job in Arabia. It was an issue for Abraham in Chaldea. It was an issue in ancient India, Japan, Germany and Polynesia, and many other parts of the world according to ancient tradition. Most ancient peoples had something in terms of astrally-oriented architecture such as sun dials, sun caves, temples designed in favor of eclipses, solar discs made of gold, and similar items. The Tower of Babel reportedly contained an astral temple at the climax. And so many ancient peoples had their astronomer-priests, astrologers, star-gazers, or a similar collection of persons who pretended to know something of future events.

Abraham protested against pantheizing the planets. What was his award for this protest? Apparently it was a one-way ticket to the Wild West of that day, Palestine.

> For which doctrines, when the Chaldeans, and the people of Mesopotamia, raised a tumult against him, he thought fit to leave that country; and at the command, and by the assistance of God, he came and lived in the land of Canaan.[4]

Interestingly enough, Josephus draws from a Babylonian named Berosus for the following comment about Abraham:

> In the tenth generation after the flood, there was among the Chaldeans a man, righteous, and great, and skillful in *celestial science*.[5] (Italics ours.)

Again, Josephus describes Abraham and his temporary visit into Egypt in a rather interesting manner in terms of intellectual pursuits:

> . . . He was admired by them, in those conferences as a very wise man, and one of great sagacity, when he discoursed on any subject he undertook; and this not only in understanding it, but in persuading other men also to assent to him. He communicated to them arithmetic, and delivered to them the science of astronomy; for before Abram came into Egypt they were unacquainted with those parts of learning, for that science came from the Chaldeans into Egypt, and from thence to the Greeks also.[6]

For what value it may contain, Josephus reports that the Chaldean engineers who constructed the ziggurats including the Tower

---

[4]Whiston, *op. cit.*, p. 95.
[5]*Ibid.*
[6]*Op. cit.*, p. 96.

of Babel did not, like many modern uniformitarians, debate the issue of whether or not there had been a great, devastating flood. They merely debated the issue of whether or not there might be another, and if so, they might rather badly need a place to flee, a place of great height on the flat, Mesopotamian plain; thus the ziggurats, which were pitched with bitumen, as was Noah's ark "that it might be liable to admit water."[7] And perhaps in their anticipated crisis, there might be further need for astronomical measurements and placations, thus the astral temples at the top of the towers. This gives something of the cosmology of Chaldea in general, and of Abraham the non-conformist. Now we shall ask a broader question, "Were the Chaldeans very uniformitarian in their thinking?"

With this we shall return our attention to Job 38, and part of the Lord's speech, a section which may contain some rather profound items on natural history and on natural science (verse 29).

Out of whose womb came the ice?

(This will be our key question, or crystallizing thought in the next chapter, relative to the Flood and the Ice Epoch, even as the key thought in this chapter is, "Speak to the earth, and it shall teach thee.")

> Out of whose womb came the ice? And the hoary frost of heaven, who hath gendered it?
> The waters are hid [or congealed like] as with a stone, and the face of the deep is frozen.
> [The discussion turns from the subject of the frozen face of the deep again toward themes astronomical.]
> Canst thou bind the sweet influences of Pleiades, or loose the bands of Orion?
> Canst thou bring forth Mazzaroth in his season?
> [Some scholars maintain that "mazzaroth" literally may mean "bearded star." Again this is related to the seeming issue of regularity or irregularity in the solar system.]
> Or canst thou guide Arcturus with his sons?
> [This is another phrase, laden with implications, of which brief note will be included in a few minutes.] [And now we come to the pervading issue of this chapter, or of this book and indeed the pervading or overriding issue of all of earth history.]
> Knowest thou the ordinances of heaven? Canst thou set the dominion thereof in the earth?
> [Paraphrased, Canst thou establish the application thereof to the earth?] (Job 38).

[7]Whiston, *op. cit.*, p. 88–89.

With this key question about the ordinances of heaven, we shall turn to the second part of this chapter, the ordinances of man. The cosmology of Job has briefly been sketched with its catastrophism and its astronomical or celestial orientation.

Part II. The Ordinances of Man

The ordinances of heaven and their application to the earth in the frame of history is the point of issue. Uniformitarians in particular, and anti-spiritual scholars in general have maintained that the planets and their satellites have been revolving in their current orbits for millions, if not billions of years. They have been maintaining this for the last 150 years, or perhaps 200 years, a rather limited span of time. This has been since the days of Kant, Laplace, Hutton and Lyell, who maintained, on the basis of their authority, that the planets have been revolving for that long. Why? Their reason is based on the fact that the nebular hypothesis, originated by Kant, so requires.

Uniformitarianism, we maintain, is the ordinance of man, and anti-spiritual man at that. This lecture is to contrast in your thinking just exactly what may be the difference between the "ordinances of heaven" (in terms of Job's cosmology and the "ordinances of man" in terms of uniformitarianism).

Uniformitarianism is the notion of "oceans of time for everything" in earth history; however it takes many forms. One form is the astronomical form, and the Nebular Hypothesis, first proposed by Immanuel Kant in 1755, and later by Laplace. Another form is the geological form, geological uniformitarianism, and the geological time scale, as proposed first by Hutton and expanded by Lyell. A third form is the biological form, Darwinism, as set forth by such figures as Darwin and Huxley. Whether in astronomy, in geology, in biology or in other areas, uniformitarianism requires time in vast increments, and assumes the same.

Kant first formulated the uniformitarian hypothesis in 1755, in his work, *General History of Nature and Theory of the Heavens*, when he was thirty-one years old. He had been raised in the Pietist Lutheran tradition in Germany. He swerved sharply from this tradition toward an agnostic and intellectual tradition in his early twenties. He taught mathematics, astronomy and physical geography prior to developing this hypothesis. After it, he went on to develop a professional skepticism and he became the leading figure in German rationalism. He originated the school of higher criticism which has been so heavily used against the evangelical and Biblical viewpoint.

Kant never declared himself to be an atheist; he claimed to be an agnostic. Notice in his hypothesis, he presumes if there is a Creator, He wound up the solar system some two billion years ago, and went away, and left it. While Kant declared for agnosticism, many of his students declared for open atheism. And from this school of German rationalism develop such thinkers as Hegel and Nietzsche, who strongly influenced Hitler. Feuerbach, another atheist, along with Hegel strongly influenced Marx, who influenced Lenin. This gives you something of the heritage of Kantianism, a sort of Pandora's Box.

In the eighteenth century in Europe, anti-spiritual scholars, atheists and agnostics, found themselves pretty consistently on the defensive. That was an era of relatively strong Christian thought, when such anti-spiritual scholars would consistently find themselves faced with the issue of the Deluge, or Flood.

They might refute the idea. But then, at the same time, people were finding fossils in every nation in Europe. A German soldier found some twenty mammoths in a bed near the Neckar River, some twenty feet below the surface. Others were finding fossils below sea level in the coal mines of Germany or Wales. Sometimes the fossils were small and sometimes their size was quite impressive. Hippopotamuses were found in England, marine crustaceans were found in the Alps, ten thousand feet and twelve thousand feet above sea level.

People would say that this was caused by the Flood. Cuvier taught that there had been great inundations several times in earth history. Atheists, in endeavoring to refute the Flood, or creation, or moral responsibility, were in a difficult plight. They badly needed some hypothesis which was simultaneously anti-Genesis and was seemingly scientific. And in the hypothesis of uniformitarianism, they found that for which they were seeking, a proposition which was simultaneously anti-Genesis and *seemingly* scientific.

Perhaps Voltaire is a good example of that era. Any mention of the Flood and its implications of judgment brought his ire and ridicule. And then someone found a fossil practically in his back yard, and he practically had apoplexy.

But with the coming of uniformitarianism, based on Kant's nebular hypothesis, Christianity suddenly became "anti-scientific" because the nebular hypothesis and uniformitarianism were equated to "science." Uniformitarianism was embraced and propagated with enthusiasm, but it remained an assumption, one which is rarely questioned. And when it is questioned, such questions are squelched or relegated to limbo by the uniformitarian establishment because somehow, the status quo, especially this status quo, seems sacrosanct.

This chapter will not take time to examine the radical inconsistencies of the nebular hypothesis in astronomy, but they are massive and severe.[8] But one will be mentioned, one among a large number. There was supposedly a gaseous nebular which condensed into the sun. A few globules did not make it into the center, inexplicably, but they cooled and formed planets. Now the planets happen to contain 98 per cent of the motion of our solar system, and but 1 per cent of the mass. This is a very thorny incongruity within the uniformitarian approach. Other problems relate to orbits of satellites, orbits of planets, retrogradely revolving moons, planes of satellites, ecliptic planes, tilts of axes, etc. When the entire proposition is meticulously examined, the nebular hypothesis explains very little, if indeed anything about origins of the planets, satellites, asteroids, meteor streams and comets.

However, students throughout the world are taught, almost without exception, that mountains were uplifted gradually, and in a time frame of tens or hundreds of millions of years ago, slowly but surely. This writer was taught this early in his college career, at the same time, incidentally, while he began to read the Scriptures. There was a differential in viewpoint to be sure, but the degree or the totality of the difference became apparent only gradually.

Part III.   Mechanics of Orogenesis (Mountain Uplifts)

Uniformitarianism never made much sense, so questions were asked. Why were dinosaurs quickly drowned and buried in sediments? Why were mammoths quickly drowned in North America, and quick-frozen or flash frozen in Siberia, even with sub-tropical vegetation in their mouths and stomachs? Why were petrified forests found one hundred miles from the South Pole by Admiral Byrd? Why were land mammals found fossilized in locations below sea level, and why were sea animals found fossilized at high elevations? More questions were asked, and there were no uniformitarian answers to these really elementary and basic issues. Meanwhile Genesis and Job began to be read.

And then more questions were asked concerning Genesis and the Flood. How was the ark floated, if the Deluge story were valid? Was the ark nearly as large as the Queen Mary in water

---

[8]Donald W. Patten, *The Biblical Flood and the Ice Epoch*, Seattle: Pacific Meridian Publishing Co., pp. 27–50, 268–308.

displacement, if not in configuration? If so, how could even a swollen river system in the Middle East float it? And even if it could, would not such a flotation be downstream, and in the direction of open sea or the wide ocean?

Why is every continent covered with sedimentary strata indicating (a) sudden, (b) massive, and (c) repeated inundations? Why are fossil chrinoids found scattered across the semi-arid Middle West when they must grow in a habitat at least 500, and up to 6,000, feet *below* sea level? Did it rain for 40 days and nights? If so, how was the ark floated for 150 days, and why are the waters described as continually rising for 150 days? Why is the Deluge story repeated in various ways throughout the cultures and nations of both hemispheres? This is but a brief sampling of questions which may be raised, questions which merit solid explanation.

By rejecting modern uniformitarian thought, one is prepared to consider the subject of earth history in terms of sudden upheavals, or catastrophes, the evidences of which are manifold. By a brief study of the solar system, one is reminded of the possibility of much cosmic chaos. And by a brief study of Genesis and Job, one is reminded of the astronomically-oriented cosmologies of the ancients.

With this line of approach, we may recall that many of the events of the Bible such as the Flood have been severely questioned and criticized, always in the "garb of scholardom" and never in the "rags of prejudice." The walls of Jericho according to uniformitarian thought could never have suddenly collapsed (although it was subsequently realized that Jericho is located astride one of the major fault zones of the earth.) And with Kant's uniformitarian rationalism, the sun and moon never could have suddenly stopped in their celestial procession, because the nebular hypothesis contained no room for such a possibility (Joshua 10:11-13; Judges 5:20; II Kings 20:11). And the Flood, the Noachian Flood, could never have occurred, except as a local flooding river system, because rain just could not accomplish a phenomenon of that magnitude. In the name of scholardom, and all that is rational, it just could not be.

Part IV. A Brief View of Our Solar System

Let us take just a brief journey out to the nearer stars in our galaxy. Among the twenty-nine nearest known stars, there are but thirteen star systems. This is because most of the sun's neighbors are binaries. A binary is two or more stars which revolve around each other, or more technically, around a point containing nothing. The sun's second-closest neighbor, Barnard's Star, is a two-body binary with one of the two stars being dark and the other luminous. Planets are suspected in the Barnard Star system also. The sun's nearest neighbor is a group of three interacting stars known as Alpha Centauri, Beta Centauri and Proxima Centauri. Alpha and Beta revolve around a common point; we may roughly say they revolve around each other. And the more remote Proxima revolves around the revolving inner two.

Let us now envision a comet such as Halley's Comet, approaching the sun, a unitary star. It turns on the sun and returns to its original distant location (its aphelion). Its orbit is stable. But consider a comet approaching the center of a binary system, with its two or more components. Consider the turning and weaving, the wobbling which would occur. Such disturbing influences result in perturbations, changes in an orbit.

Now let us briefly look at Pluto, which approaches the sun at a distance of about 2.7 billion miles and retreats to 4.5 billion miles. At perihelion (its closest approach to the sun), Pluto is 35 million miles nearer in than is Neptune. Pluto's year is about 248 of our years. Thus once every 2½ centuries, Neptune suddenly becomes the outermost planet, the ninth planet for a brief season. The eccentricity of Pluto's orbit is a phenomenon which has lead astronomers to widely suspect that Pluto and Neptune may have interacted historically.

Neptune's two satellites revolve in retrograde motion (the only two major satellites in our solar system with retrograde motion.) Halley's Comet has retrograde motion, and Halley's Comet turns (has its turn point) in the region of Neptune's orbit. Nereid's orbit is extremely eccentric, and it looks as if it almost escaped the Neptune system whereas Halley's Comet possibly did. This whole system of Neptune, Pluto, Nereid, Triton, Halley's Comet and other comets is suggestive that great disturbances of perturbations have occurred in the vicinity of Neptune at some time in the past. This is an example of suspected gravitational interaction some 2.5 billion miles distant from the earth, a fairly remote example, by most standards.

Next, let us briefly examine the region of Saturn, with its brilliant rings. It has been known for nearly 300 years that Saturn's Rings were bands, some 41,500 miles wide, and some 180,000 miles in diameter. In 1948, they were first measured in terms of thickness; they are 10 miles thick. From this modest thickness, plus the known reflectivity of Saturn's Rings, it was immediately realized that the rings must be composed of ice particles, and not rock particles as are the asteroids and the meteor streams.

In astronomy, if two bodies were to approach, the gravitational interaction would increase in magnitude, and in geometric proportions relative to distance. (The inverse of the square of the distance.) If they were to approach to a distance of 2.44 times the radius of the larger, the internal gravity of the smaller would be overcome, and it would fragmentize at approximately this distance, assuming the two bodies are of similar density. This distance is known as *Roche's Limit*. It is generally suspected that some icy celestial wanderer came too close to Saturn at some time in the past. It came so close that it passed Roche's Limit and fragmentized. The result was a vast catastrophe, in this case, an icy catastrophe; the remains are Saturn's Rings.

This is another example of gravitational interaction, of a greater magnitude than the circumstances surrounding perturbations in the Neptune, Pluto, Nereid, Triton complex. Yet Saturn is some 800,-000,000 miles distant from the earth, a location which is yet rather remote by most standards.

Coming in closer, one passes the orbit of Jupiter and moves into the belt of asteroids, battered fragments of a former planet. In the case of Saturn's Rings, the body causing the fragmentation is obvious, Saturn. In the case of the asteroids, the body causing the fragmentation is not obvious, for it is no longer revolving within the zone of asteroids.

Coming in closer to the earth, one passes the region of Mars. Mariner has revealed that Mars does not possess canals; however it does possess craters, and they are astonishingly numerous, and many are astonishingly large. In fact they are so numerous that there are craters superimposed on craters, which are superimposed on craters in a triple overlay. To quote a phrase by Prof. Talmage Wilson of Seattle, it would appear likely that Mars has had one or two bad nights out. Further, there are circumstances relating to the two minuscule moons, Deimos and Phobos, which are further indicative of perturbed orbits, gravitational interaction and celestial catastrophism within the Mars system.[9]

Mars, Deimos and Phobos are some 40,000,000 miles from the earth, a distance which is not very great in astronomical terms. But is this the closest location where evidences of ancient catastrophism exist? The closest body to the earth is the moon, its binary partner, some 240,000 miles distant. Is the moon also pocked with numerous craters? The answer is, yes, and some of them are 150 miles in diameter. Further, our space probes indicate that the

[9]Patten, *op cit.*, pp. 183-192. There may be a correlation in ancient. literature between Arcturus and its sons, Ares and its steeds, and Mars with its legendary Deimos and Phobos.

back side of the moon, which earthians never see, is pocked with craters more numerous than is the moon's face.

Catastrophism in the realm of Neptune, some 2.6 billion miles distant is one thing; catastrophism in the realm of Saturn, some .8 billion miles may be much the same in terms of magnitude, but catastrophism in terms of the earth's nearest neighbors, in one case only 240,000 miles distant, this is catastrophism of quite a different dimension. There are ample evidences of celestial catastrophism in the solar system, and there is little reason to suppose that the earth has escaped.

It might be noted at this point, for future reference, that the moon not only contains craters. It also contains mountain systems which have a similar pattern to the scallop-like or arcuate uplift patterns of the mountains on the earth. In fact they also rise to similar elevations.

Part V.   A View of the Deluge in Terms of a Celestial Catastrophe

Many of us have assumed that the Flood was caused by rain because it rained for forty days and nights as the flood commenced. However, it may be that while the rain was simultaneous with the Flood, it may not be the cause; it may be just a little addition. In geography, there are what are termed "cause and effect relationships," but there are other relationships which are termed "associative relationships." For instance, corn and pumpkins both ripen in the autumn; however, the ripening of corn does not cause the ripening of pumpkins; they are both dependent on other factors which affect both in common: the seasons. This is an "associative relationship."

Genesis teaches that it rained for 40 days and nights; however Genesis also teaches that the water rose for 150 days and nights. Thus, if rain were the only cause factor of the Flood, there are 110 days which are involved with little or no rain. Moreover Genesis teaches that the waters increased, and increased continually.

Genesis also teaches that the ark did not end up near the sea shore or an ocean shore. Today if a large boat comes to the end of its days, it is usually at the end of a dock or pier. But this, the most famous barge of ancient times, did not come to rest at the edge of any sea shore. Perhaps the second most important vessel of ancient times was the Argo piloted by Jason; it presumably came to its end somewhere on the shores of the Aegean, or possibly the Black Sea.

Diagram, LOCATION OF THE ARK
The Heartland Region of the Eastern Hemisphere

But the ark came to its final resting place some ten thousand feet above sea level, far from the shores of any sea, be it the Black, the Aegean, the Red, the Mediterranean or any other sea. Today, in the Puget Sound country near Seattle, we have ferry boats plying across the sound. However if we were to take a hike high up into the Cascades, this is about the last place one would expect to find a ferry boat. Yet such is the resting place of this large barge, the ark. This is remarkable to say the least. The resting place of the ark is reported to be in the Armenian Mountains, in the region of Mt. Ararat. The Armenian Mountains comprise a mountain complex or a "knot," located near the heart of Eurasia.

This is utterly inexplicable in terms of viewing the Flood as caused by rain. For instance, rain is substantially caused by evaporating ocean water, and rain usually falls in its greater proportions in marine locations. This location, the Armenian Mountains, is about fifteen hundred miles from the Indian Ocean, about two thousand miles from the Arctic Ocean, about three thousand miles from the Atlantic Ocean and about five thousand miles from the Pacific. To say the least, it is hardly a marine location.

In fact, it is in a zone called the horse latitudes where deserts are much more common than are forests, a zone where, by and large, it just does not rain very much. The Armenian region is surrounded by regions of deserts and steppes including such deserts as the Arabian, Saharan and Nubian deserts to the west, and the Gobi and Sinkiang Deserts to the east. To the north are the deserts and steppelands of Turkestan, Uzbekistan and Kazakhstan, and to the south and west are the dry interior plateaus of Anatolia and Iran. By and large, this is a region where it just does not rain very much. Yet this is the region where the ark was grounded.

Some theologians have endeavored to explain the flood in terms of a period of prolonged cyclonic storms and intense rain. Their endeavor, be it very sincere, has been to reconcile Genesis to uniformitarianism. However it just makes no sense geographically, and it seems to make little sense theologically.

In reviewing the story of the Deluge, one also comes upon the interesting observation that the fountains of the great deep began to surge forth, and continued in their surging for 150 days. Now if we view the Flood in terms of a gravitational interaction, a celestial catastrophe, then we may think in terms of tides, tides of subcontinental dimensions, tides which could perhaps float an ark or any other type of driftwood to an elevation of many thousand feet above sea level.

Tidal movement is related not only to gravitational interaction, but also to the rotation of the earth. The earth becomes somewhat football-shaped, or egg-shaped, due to the stresses of gravitational interaction. There are two nodes or high tides, one facing the extra-terrestrial center of gravity, and the other directly opposite to it. On the rim region, there is a zone of low tides.

Thus there are two high tides daily, actually every 24½ hours to be more accurate, and two low tides also daily. Genesis says that the waters increased continually, something which is quite similar to describing of tidal activity, which also increases daily, and twice daily.

When I was a youngster in Montana, I noticed in the late summer that the tumbleweeds would dry up, and begin to blow with the warm August breezes. They would bounce and roll, and roll and bounce until they became caught, perhaps on some barbed wire, perhaps on a snow fence or some sage brush. Perhaps we can view the ark somewhat similarly, as being floated on the Flood chaos until it finally became caught, and caught at high tide in a hedge of mountains. The Armenian Knot region happens to be the second highest knot complex in the Eastern Hemisphere, next to the Pamir Knot where the mighty Himalayas, the Karakorums, the Tien Shans and the Kun Luns all meet.

Thus if we look at the flood in terms of tides rather than rain, many things become far more logical and this includes the manner of flotation, the direction of flotation, the 150 day period of gravitational crisis, the daily increasing of waters, and several other features.

With tides five thousand and ten thousand feet high sweeping the earth daily, sedimentation and stratification would suddenly become great factors reshaping the surface of the earth. Tides ten thousand feet high will create pressures, two tons per square inch and more, pressures which would fossilize animals and petrify forests in a matter of hours.

In a quarry in England a tree was found, about one hundred feet long, and at a forty degree angle. It went through strata after strata, each supposedly laid down millions of years apart. At the top, the tree was about one foot in diameter. At the bottom it was five feet in one diameter and two feet in the other diameter, as if it had come under immense pressures. Obviously if the strata were laid down millions of years apart, the top would have long since rotted. This is but one of thousands of inexplicable items for uniformitarianism to explain; in my opinion the understanding of the Flood in its cosmological perspective helps immensely.

Part VI. The Uplifting of Mountain Systems

If we consider the Flood to be tidal in nature and a result of gravitational interaction, a celestial catastrophe, then we must follow through and realize that not only one of the earth's three fluids, but rather all three would be in tidal movement simultaneously. This includes the air (the atmosphere), the oceans (the hydrosphere), and the magma (the lava or the fluid part of the lithosphere).

There is an interesting perspective in Genesis concerning the animals coming onto the ark several days before the fulness of the chaos enveloped and floated the ark. I notice by way of coincidence that animals have a strange way of sensing seismic disturbances before they occur. Perhaps they can feel the micro shocks or the micro vibrations.

In Madison County, Montana, there was a severe earthquake in 1959. This was near Yellowstone Park. Rangers in the area noticed birds migrating out of the area the day *before* the earthquake occurred.

In 1924 there was a severe earthquake in Honshu, Japan. It was very destructive. It was predicted by an old Buddhist priest, who understood from tradition that a certain species of fish acted strangely before earthquakes. (Japan is located in the zone of earthquake activity and volcanism known as the Pacific Rim of Fire.) He predicted it would be a particularly severe earthquake because the fish had been acting strangely for months.

In 1902 Mt. Pelee on Martinique blew up. Martinique is one of the islands of the Lesser Antilles in the Caribbean. The day before this happened, an old Negro sheepherder noticed his sheep on the side of the mountain in an extremely disturbed state. He made his way to the mayor of St. Pierre, and said that something dreadful was about to happen. The mayor did not take the muttering old sheepherder very seriously; however the next day forty thousand people were engulfed in hot, incandescently hot gases and falling cinders. The animals apparently had anticipated this catastrophe, perhaps by feeling the early micro shocks of the event.

I note, by way of comparison, the remarkably strange behavior of the animals the week before the Deluge. If we understand that the lava within the earth's crust was beginning to heave and ebb, we can begin to perceive the seismic chaos, and the seismic crescendo which was approaching.

We consider the oceans as vast. They contain some 280,000,000 to 300,000,000 cubic miles of water, ample to float an ark 5,000 feet above mean sea level, if in marked tidal upheaval. Some uniformitarians and some theistic evolutionists have rejected the Flood story because, they suppose, rain just couldn't achieve such a phenomenon, and up to a point, they may be right.

However tides which can swamp a sandcastle at the sea shore

might also be able to swamp the Alps, the Andes, the Pyrenees or the Ararats. It is merely a matter of magnitude. It is not the lack of a mechanism.

If the oceans are vast, they are vast only when compared to smaller features. When compared to the ocean of lava within the earth's crust, the hydrosphere might be described as "peanuts." The earth's crust is from five to thirty miles thick, about as thick relatively as an onionskin to an onion, or a layer of paper to a globe. Within that is heavy, hot, plastic-like, viscous magma, reaching deep toward the core of the earth. There is evidence that the center of the earth may contain a core, perhaps one thousand miles in diameter of a more solid material.

But essentially on the inside of the earth's crust one finds an ocean of lava, or magma. This magma has a volume relationship to the oceans of about 5000:1. Moreover it is much heavier, cubic foot per cubic foot, than is water. Its weight compared to the hydrosphere is about 30,000:1. And this mass, we must consider, was also in tidal upheaval during the Flood crisis period.

Fluids, when in tidal activity, tend to amplify their force if they are enclosed or contained. Whereas normal tides may be from two to six feet on the open ocean, tides in higher latitudes and along continental shelves are amplified. The Bay of Fundy experiences tides as high as fifty and fifty-five feet; the Thames Estuary approaching London experiences tides of well over thirty feet. This is an example of amplification of tidal force by constriction. Within the earth's crust, we may view the entire ocean of magma as constricted; hence we may view the potential thrust force not in terms of tons per square inch, as we measured compression of the oceans, but rather the force of upthrust might well be megatons per square inch, the very magnitude of forces which are required to uplift mountain systems.

This writer comes from the high plains of Montana, near the majestic sawtooth ranges of Glacier Park and the Canadian Rockies. When he was a teen-ager, he worked in the forest service. He stood on top of the Bitterroot Divide and viewed the mountain systems as they stretched for 100 miles and more into Idaho on the right, and other ranges as they stretched for 100 and 150 miles toward the high horizon in Montana. He noticed the pattern, a pattern resembling the branches of a Christmas tree in relation to the stock. This is known in geography as a dendritic pattern. He has viewed the Continental Divide and the mountain ranges and peaks associated therewith.

When he arrived in college, the issue of uniformitarianism was presented relative to mountain uplifts. Millions of years for this and that were constantly and casually tossed around. But it never did make sense. With his geographical background, he furthermore knew that these patterns of mountains, and their apparent recentness and violence, recurred, spanning all the continents. Without going into the many factors and propositions of diastrophism, we may be safe in saying that all uniformitarian explanations for mountain systems are based, either consciously or subconsciously, on Lyellian thought. They all assume (1) millions, tens and hundreds of millions of years for orogenetical development, (2) causation is from the downward direction, anywhere from twenty to two thousand miles downward, and (3) all uplifts are local in scope relative to any given year or any given millennium.

On the other hand, if one postulates tides in the oceans, he must simultaneously postulate tides, and far greater tides within the magma. Thus he must view the earth's thin crust as being in a sort of bellows-like activity, tortured from without (by water compression, sedimentation and stratification) and from within (by faulting, fracturing and upthrusting) all simultaneously. Beyond this, there is also the atmospheric factor, and a dabble of rain also involved. All three fluids were simultaneously in upheaval. This then means that not only was the ark uplifted by oceanic tides, but also the Armenian Mountains, along with many others were uplifted by magma tides simultaneously. Hence Mt. Ararat may well have not existed before the Flood.

Concerning the scope of the Flood, with the following diagram, you can view the pattern of recent mountain systems, and ask yourself whether or not this pattern is global or local. In the writer's view, it is a "dead ringer" for a pattern of celestial catastrophism, gravitational interaction acting upon a rotating sphere. Notice there were two zones of uplift; this is suggestive that there were two crisis periods or crescendos during this 150 days and nights of geophysical chaos.

Concerning mountain uplifts, let us look at little Switzerland and its Alps. Switzerland is among the smallest countries in Europe, which itself is a small continent. Switzerland is about eight times as large as Harris County; it is about three times as large as Pecos County. It contains perhaps 15,000 square miles, which is something less than 1/100 of 1 per cent of the land surface of the earth.

Yet within the Alps are such mountain uplifts as the Carnic Alps, the Bernese Alps, the Jura Alps and the Rhaetian Alps, each range uplifted tens of millions of years earlier or later than its neighboring range. Thus uniformitarianism requires each uplift to be local in scope, for any given year. However the pattern is global, and it is suspected that 100 per cent of the inside of the earth's crust was involved in upheaval, and not just a tiny portion, such as a fraction of 1/100 of 1 per cent. This gives some perspective of scope of mountain uplifts, global or local. Herein lies a differential of 99.9+ per cent in terms of scope and perspective.

Secondly, the catastropic view is that mountain uplifts occurred about 5,000 years ago, at least as far as these particular cycles, the Alpine-Himalayan, and the Circum-Pacific are concerned. Uniformitarian thinking places the dating in the region of 160,000,000 years ago, give or take 30,000,000 years. Herein lies a differential of 99.996+ per cent in terms of timing and perspective.

Thirdly, relative to direction of causation, all of the various uniformitarian propositions, regardless of their general vagueness, have supposed that the cause was downward, generally straight downward. In the catastrophic perspective, the direction of causation was straight upward.

When I was in the army, we had target practice on the firing range. If we missed the target by a few seconds, it was poor shooting. If we missed by a minute, it was wild shooting. But if we missed the target by 180°, that was unthinkable. But this, in my opinion, is the achievement of uniformitarianism. They have attributed the cause of orogenesis as being straight downward, and they have made an error in the proportions of 180°. This may be called the perfect error. (Some people say there is no such thing as a perfect error, but if there is, Lyell, with his geological uniformitarian hypothesis, has made it.)

Again, in terms of distance of causation, uniformitarianism has suggested that the cause of mountain uplifts were between twenty and two thousand miles deep within the earth's crust. Beyond their error in direction, their error in distance is probably something in the neighborhood of twenty thousand to thirty thousand miles, again an error in the general magnitude of 99 per cent.

In much scientific experimentation, an error tolerance of 1/10 of 1 per cent, or 1/10 of a degree is much too great. However uniformitarianism, masquerading as if it were science, has seemingly made an error of about 180°, and then has pointed to Christianity, and Genesis, and has claimed, in the name of scholardom to be sure, that the Genesis record is unscientific. And with their claims, they have not only represented Genesis as unscientific; they have taken over the curriculums of the classrooms and texts of the entire civilization, and have influenced no doubt millions of students away from the kingdom of God.

Uniformitarianism may be somewhat of a joke in terms of the

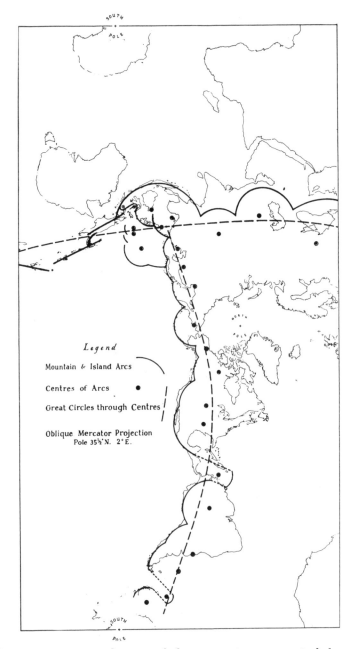

The primary arcs or elements of the two active orogenetic belts, connected like a series of scallops.

J. Tuzo Wilson, *The Earth as a Planet,* ed., Kuiper, Chicago, Illinois: University of Chicago Press, p. 153.

magnitude of its error, and in terms of its lamentably limp explanations for some very impressive facts in earth history. But its effects, in its forms presented (including the Kantian form, the Lyellian form and the Darwinist form) have been powerful in turning literally millions away from the kingdom of God. Eternal destinies may well be involved, and that of millions. Uniformitarianism, which has made atheism virulent in our century, may be a joke, but it is a very, very bad joke indeed.

Naturally there are many facets of the Flood catastrophe which an article cannot treat. The subject is so vast that a book, much less an article, can hardly scratch the surface. However if this catastrophic approach is correct regarding the tidal nature of the Flood and its mechanism (gravitational interaction), along with its celestial perspective, then a few things need to be rethought. Some of them are listed in the following questions:

1. Has not geology become very sleepy in a philosophic sense since it fell under the uniformitarian monopoly? Are there not vast new horizons to traverse once it again awakens?
2. How many uniformitarian textbooks need rewriting, and how many uniformitarian authorities need to go back and learn some new ideas?
3. Is uniformitarianism science or is it pseudoscience and pseudohistory?
4. Did the bulk of "mesozoic" and "cenozoic" developments in earth history occur during the two crises of the Flood period, some five thousand years ago?
5. Is Christianity in general, and the Genesis record in particular, really anti-scientific?
6. Is not a global flood perspective much more coherent than a local flood view?
7. During the crisis of the Flood year, might it be said that He "removeth the mountains, and they know not" and He "shaketh the earth out of her place, and the pillars thereof tremble?"
8. Should we take Job's advice, and "speak to the earth" and rather anticipate that it will teach us well?
9. In that reportedly ungodly era prior to the Flood, who suggested or advised Noah to construct such a large barge.
10. Is it possible that uniformitarianism is the ordinance of man, and anti-spiritual man at that? And should we not know it for what it is?
11. "Knowest thou the ordinances of heaven?" "Canst thou set the dominion [the application] thereon in the earth?"
12. And in peering back not just to, but rather through the mists of the Flood era, do we not see a rather majestic creation? And in such a glimpse, do we not gain some little perspective of the majesty of our Creator?

The Ice Epoch

by Donald W. Patten

VI

THE ICE EPOCH

Out of Whose Womb Came the Ice?

(Job 38:29a)

Knowest thou the ordinances of heaven? Canst thou set the dominion [or application] thereof in the earth? (Job 38:33).

The subject of this chapter is ice, and ice in rather vast amounts (at least from our current perspectives). How much ice was involved in the Ice Epoch? Where did the ice come from? Where was it deposited? How suddenly did it appear? How rapidly did it melt off? When did it occur? Out of whose womb came the ice?

Again, we should briefly sketch traditional thinking concerning the Ice Epoch, the so-called Ice Age or Ice Ages. Within uniformitarian thought, there has been a requirement of five, six or perhaps seven Ice Ages. For instance there are rocks with attributed ages of 200,000,000 years which have striations. So there had to be an Ice Age at that time. Later, dinosaurs roamed Arctic prairies, so there had to be a recession of the ice. Dinosaurs supposedly died out about 60,000,000 years ago, and yet they were followed by mammoths, some of which were enveloped in some rather icy conditions. By the time the geological time scale is applied to the fossil data, ice ages are coming and going almost constantly in what is known as "mesozoic" and "cenozoic" time.

My understanding is that the two zones of mountain uplifts which were demonstrated did not occur 130,000,000 to 200,000,000 years ago, but rather something like 5,000 years ago, and during the same year, the year of Noah's crisis, the year of Noah's flotation. Thus uniformitarians, if they acknowledge a flood at all, will all agree that the Ice Epoch, the so-called Ice Ages occurred prior to the Flood.

Yet some rather well-oriented catastrophists, mostly fundamentalists in their view of life, men like Price, Nelson and others have noted that the Flood caused a vast amount of sedimentation, forming layer after layer of strata. And such formations have been scoured out. Their proposition has been that the Ice Epoch could not have preceded the Flood, but rather must have followed it.

119

There are a whole series of specific considerations to which we might at this time direct our attentions. Such considerations might well include such items as lateral moraines, terminal moraines, drumlins, erratic boulders, striations, drowned continental shelves, quick-frozen or flash-frozen mammoths, ice caves in lava plateaus, ice flow patterns, glacial lakes, diverted river systems and the like. But before we dig into some of these specifics, it may be well to take an imaginary airplane trip, an airplane trip during the Ice Epoch, and we may view, in our mind's eye, our imagination, the location, the dimension and the scope of this icy blanket.

All who travel today by airplane know something of aerial views, aerial views from as high as thirty thousand and forty thousand feet, a rather panoramic perspective. From Seattle to Houston, via Portland and Dallas, a distance of two thousand miles, one can see on the way the snow-encrusted extinct volcanoes known as Mt. Adams, Mt. Hood, Mt. Rainier and Mt. St. Helens.

Let us imagine another plane trip, a non-stop flight, a distance of about fifty-five hundred miles. In our imaginary flight, we embark just south of the flowing edge of the ice mass, at a location where the mighty Columbia and the Willamette meet, now known as Portland. We fly north about eighty miles, and we begin to see the edge of the ice mass in some broad tongues, near what is to-day Chehalis, Washington.

We proceed into the Puget Sound Country, but there is no Puget Sound; sea level is perhaps three hundred to four hundred feet below the current level, and has not flooded Puget Sound. Puget Sound is merely a valley of ice, with its bottom being deeply scoured out. In fact there are a whole series of valleys of ice, with occasional lateral and terminal moraines in the process of formation, moraines some five hundred and nearly one thousand feet high, stretching like long ridges around the ice flows.

Our airplane climbs, and we proceed across the icy Cascades where a whole series of fresh volcanoes are belching out their smoke and lava. Crossing British Columbia, hundreds of rugged mountain peaks are dotted among the ever-increasing blanket of ice, many half-buried, and some almost completely buried.

Then we cross the majestic Rockies, with their knife-like saw-tooth faces. And we see our last mountain peak. Crossing Alberta and Northern Saskatchewan, we see nothing but dazzling, blue-white ice, in one, vast, unbroken landscape.

As our plane crosses into the Northwest Territories, it rises to seventeen thousand feet in altitude. It has to rise or it will crash into the ice mass, the so-called Keewatin Node, located east of Great Slave Lake. And then our airplane passes other nodes such as the

Labrador Node, of a similar elevation. Crossing Davis Strait, leaving Baffin Island, and approaching Greenland, our plane drops a little in altitude, for the ice mass is not quite so deep; nevertheless no ocean is seen, and no Greenland is seen. Only ice appears in a vast, unbroken blue-white blanket of ice. This is all that is visible of Iceland.

Proceeding eastward, a ridge of mountains appears, on what is today known as the Fenno-Scandinavian Shield. Eastward and southward, one crosses southern Sweden and the Baltic Regions, and suddenly a hill or two come into view, poking their ridges out from the blanket of ice. Flying deeper into Germany and Poland, tongues of ice are seen now between ranges of hills. Glistening rivers are draining off vast volumes of melt water. And shortly, little ice is seen, except in the Alpine regions. The ice mass has been spanned. Our plane trip covered some fifty-five hundred miles, and apart from some mountain ranges and volcanic cones, it was one, vast, mass of shifting, flowing ice, from one continent to another.

In our plane trip we crossed not only the top of the ice mass, but we also passed the magnetic pole almost directly. But we did not come within twelve hundred miles of the geographical pole.

We saw a mass of ice which may have included eight million to ten million cubic miles of frozen water. And apparently a similar amount was located in the Antarctic Region. This is a lot of ice to see. It is a lot of water to refrigerate. It requires many septillion calories of heat exchange. And it would appear to this writer that such catastrophists as Nelson and Price were correct when they deduced that this vast icy view, this vast icy mass, was formed, or at least flowed out after the Flood. Correction. We do not say it was formed after the Flood, but it did outflow after the Flood. Again we repeat the question, "Out of whose womb came the ice?" (Job 39:29). And its corollary question is also brought to attention, paraphrasing Job 39:30. "When were the waters congealed like a stone, and when was the face of the deep frozen?"

With this vast icy perspective in mind, and this great cosmological question asked, it may be time to begin reviewing some of the perspectives and circumstances, circumstances which individually are pieces of this great puzzle in earth history.

Requirement No. 1
The Location of the Ice Mass

It has already been noted that the ice mass was centered, strangely enough, not over the geographical north pole where so little sunlight falls. Rather it was centered over the magnetic pole, some twelve hundred miles distant.

The location of the ice mass was about fifty-two hundred miles in diameter; its depth was about three miles in thickness. It might be viewed like an icy pancake, a blanket which was slightly deeper in the center than elsewhere, and its depth feathered out toward the edge or the periphery. The location of the ice mass was rather eccentric to, say, the location of the Arctic Circle. Figure 1 demonstrates this.

Today, Northern Siberia is the coldest place on earth, with the possible exception of the offshore islands north of Siberia. These islands, along with Antarctica, are the two regions on earth today which are truly uninhabitable. Yet these islands were not glaciated by the ice mass; they were not covered by the ice mass. This area today contains some rather handsome, flash-frozen mammoths and rhinos, some with apparently subtropical types of vegetation and humid temperate types of vegetation in their stomachs, yet undigested, and in their mouths, yet unswallowed. Trees with pine cones are found quick-frozen, as are elderberry trees with ripe berries. But this region was not glaciated.

The ice mass just did not bear the same geographical pattern as do, say, annual isotherms or monthly isotherms today. For instance in Washington, Chehalis, latitude 47° N., was glaciated, whereas Novaya Zemlya, latitude 75° N., was mostly not glaciated. Lakes Erie and Michigan, latitude 42° N., were scooped out by the tongues of the flowing ice mass; yet Bennett Island, the northernmost of the New Siberian Islands, was left apparently unscathed by glaciation at the time of the Ice Epoch. Bennett Island has a latitude of 76° N.

And in central Illinois, Indiana, and Ohio, the ice mass flowed to a latitude of 39° N. latitude, more than half of the way to the equator. Yet Severnaya Zemlya (Northern Land), latitude 79°, was hardly touched. This geographical location bears an associative relationship to the magnetic poles, as well as to the Aurora Borealis. But its geography is hardly the geography of the Arctic Circle, and the geographical north pole. Why was this so? An answer to this perplexing problem will be developed later in this chapter.

Requirement No. 2
The Volume of the Ice Mass

How much ice was contained in this ice blanket, or ice sheet? We have already suggested the answer, which lies between fifteen

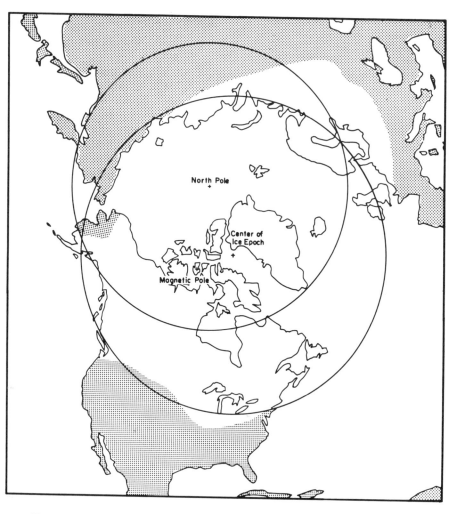

Figure 1 – THE GEOGRAPHICAL LOCATION OF THE ICE
EPOCH IN THE NORTHERN HEMISPHERE

with regard to   (1)   the Geographical Center of the Ice Age
(2)   the Geographical North Pole
(3)   the Magnetic North Pole

million and twenty million cubic miles of ice for the two ice sheets
located over both magnetic (and geographical) poles. There apparently was perhaps eight million to ten million cubic miles of
ice in the northern ice sheet.

This is a lot of ice. If it were spread evenly across the planet, it would make a layer about four hundred feet deep. Think of four hundred blocks of ice, each one foot cubed, stacked upon a small desk. This gives you an idea of the amount of ice which is required to explain the Ice Epoch. And it gives you an idea of the magnitude of refrigeration which is similarly required for explanation.

Requirement No. 3
The Depth of the Ice Mass

Our next question, or rather perspective, concerns the depth of the ice mass. This was between fifteen thousand and seventeen thousand feet in its nodes on the Canadian Shield. Seemingly a similar amount of ice was deposited in the Antarctic Regions simultaneously.

If one, perhaps a uniformitarian, endeavors to explain this ice mass in terms of falling snowflakes, and long eons of time, he is faced with many massive problems. One concerns heat exchange. Falling snowflakes are dependent upon the evaporation of ocean water, which is dependent on heat, not refrigeration. Similarly, planetary wind systems would be needed to transport the water vapor; however, planetary wind systems are a mechanism for mixing of air, and of moderating of temperatures; both do little to contribute to a solid explanation.

In Antarctica, in 1958, a core was taken by a government team off the Ross Ice Shelf, near Little America. Knowledge was desired as to just exactly how thick or deep the sheet of ice was at that location. Drilling began at an elevation of five thousand feet above sea level on the crust of the ice. Drilling proceeded for ten thousand feet, until finally bedrock was reached. The drill went through ice all the way. The meaning contained in this endeavor is that today, some five thousand years after the Flood, ice remains on bedrock, not five thousand feet above sea level, but five thousand feet *below* sea level, where it snows very, very seldom indeed.

When uniformitarian thought relies on falling snowflakes to explain the ice mass, perhaps on the Canadian Shield, such thinkers seemingly trap themselves into the position of requiring that this same phenomenon occurs some five thousand feet below sea level, and in a continuum not of water but of brine. And we all know what just a little bit of salt will do on a frozen pavement.

It may seem as if this subject of the Ice Epoch stretches from the sublime to the ridiculous. Yet any uniformitarian explanation, to be thorough and consistent, must take such a preposterous position. It is not the only ludicrous proposition in the "slow-snow" theory, but it demonstrates the need for better explanations. Again, the real question is not whether the uniformitarian approach is coherent. The real question is, "Out of whose womb came the ice."

We would bring to your attention, at this juncture, a parallelism which we cannot take time to develop; nevertheless it should be noted. In Section I, it was seen that mountain systems were raised up, in an arcuate alignment, sweeping across the surface of the earth in *Great Circle* patterns. These arcuate uplifts traversed oceanic basins equally as easily as continental massifs. Now also note that ice deposition has occurred, apparently equally as easy on oceanic basins as upon continental shields. This is a parallelism. Further note that during the Flood, if there were tides of five thousand and six thousand foot magnitudes, not only were continental massifs drowned or washed in tides, but simultaneously oceanic basins were uncovered. This may be why so much marine life is found in fossil form in hill and mountain terrain; the oceans surged forth, and their debris was swept out. Perhaps there was no such thing as "mean sea level" in the ordinary sense of the word during the period of the Flood catastrophe. Thus we bring to your attention, without further development, the rather remarkable presence of ice in hydrosphere, ice five thousand feet below sea level in an ocean of brine, remaining there even to this millennium. This is one remarkable location for ice deposition; consider another one, quite different but equally remarkable.

Requirement No. 4
The Ice Cave Phenomena of Eastern Washington

This phenomenon also occurs in Eastern Oregon and in Southern Idaho, in what is known as the Columbia Plateau, a lava plateau.

At the time of the Flood, with vast tidal forces enveloping the earth, I feel that the crust of the earth was tortured simultaneously from within (by upthrusts of lava) and from without (by oceanic tides washing around). The crust of the earth was in something like a bellows-like circumstance. Upheavals of magma occurred, squeezed up in this gravitational crisis involving our rotating planet. In some places mountain ranges were the product, a deformation of the earth's crust. In some places, lava bled through a fissure and formed a volcanic cone. In other places, lava bled through a fracture and formed a large, basaltic plateau. The Deccan Plateau in India is an example. So is the Columbia Plateau in the Pacific Northwest. Only in the region of the Columbia Plateau, incoming ice, and inflowing ice mixed with the upwelling lava in a unique commingling.

In the Pacific Northwest today, many ice caves are found. When cuts were blasted out of the volcanic hills near Grand Coulee for highways, pockets of ice were encountered. Today, Skamania County, located between the volcanic cones of Mt. Hood, Mt. St. Helens and Mt. Adams, is known to contain more than twenty ice caves. Deschutes County, Oregon, contains many ice caves, sandwiched in between lava formations.

The writer examined one ice cave about fifteen miles downstream from Grand Coulee Dam in Douglas County, on the Norman Alling ranch. This ice cave had been used for the refrigeration of beef during the hot summers when the neighbors were resigned to salt pork. Even today, the Alling family has a tradition of gathering on the fourth of July, and among the festivities is chipping some ice from the cave, several hundred yards from the house, and using it in conjunction with an old-fashioned crank-operated ice cream bucket. And ice cream is made from fresh ranch cream and ice, which must be considered to be at least five thousand years old in terms of its terrestrial existence.

As one enters this cave, he is impressed by the cold wind emanating from the cave, and the icy stalactites and stalagmites protruding from the lava formations. The fact that ice has been sandwiched in between lava formations is obvious, but it could hardly have been accomplished by falling snow flakes, even over unending eons of time. The fact that some ice has melted is obvious; such melting is the reciprocal of the caves themselves. The fact that much ice remains is also obvious, which is suggestive that the entire formation is recent in terms of millennia, and not ancient in terms of millions of years.

For instance, the climate in this region averages around 42° annually, summer and winter, day and night. The summers are sufficiently warm to grow good crops of peaches in the lower valleys, as well as other types of soft fruit. Temperatures within the earth's crust do not diminish; rather they increase, and at the rate of 16° per one thousand feet. Some fifteen thousand feet below the surface, temperatures exist which will convert water into superheated steam. And yet, within this climate, and within this lava formation, an ice cave exists.

It was inspected by Mr. Arthur Kalmen along with the writer. Mr. Kalmen was an employee of the Bureau of Indian Affairs at the time, a graduate in agriculture from Washington State College. We estimated the volume of water flow from the spring at the base of the hill. Mrs. Alling stated that Mr. Alling had taken its temperature many times during the last several decades. The temperature was always 34° F., summer or winter, day or night.

This writer estimated the rate of flow from the spring at five gallons per hour, an estimate considered quite conservative by Mr. Kalmen. And we both ignored seepage. Yet by projecting an hourly flow of five gallons into five thousand years, one must conclude that over one million tons of ice have melted and, unquestionably, much yet remains, sandwiched in between these basaltic formations. "Out of whose womb came the ice?"

Ice deposition in the hydrosphere, five thousand feet below sea level on the Antarctic Shelf is one thing, but ice deposition between lava formations is quite another thing; both require explanation. And I am convinced that if we can make correct catastrophic assumptions, and rid our thinking of our uniformitarian subconscious assumptions, a correct explanation shall not be very difficult to achieve.

Requirement No. 5
The Geometrical Pattern of the Ice

Ice today forms where snowfall exceeds melting and outflow. The result is a glacier, usually high in the mountains, but lower down in Alaska. Between seven and nine inches of snow will compress into an inch of ice. If we are going to explain fifteen thousand feet of ice, we must multiply this fifteen thousand by twelve inches, and remultiply by the seven, eight or nine factor relative to the compression of snow. The result is something over one million inches of snowfall.

Snows occur in mountainous regions where winds are forced upwards and are compelled to discharge their water vapor. This is called orographic precipitation. Another type is cyclonic precipitation, which is the result of storm fronts where cold polar air masses mix with warmer, humid, maritime air masses. The result of the mix is snow, often a blizzard.

In the Pacific Northwest, where the Cascades catch much orographic precipitation, snowfalls of ten feet are fairly common; snowfalls of fifty feet are unheard of. But concerning an explanation for the Ice Epoch, we are talking about a snowfall of hundreds of thousands of feet, and that not in a mountainous region, and not anywhere near an ocean, a source for precipitation. On the Canadian Shield, some one thousand miles from the Pacific Ocean, one locates the Keewatin Node, near the magnetic pole.

The pattern of snowfall in Antarctica today is a peripheral pattern, or a saucer-shaped pattern. Snow falls on the edges of the continent, where marine, saturated air mixes with cold polar air. But in the heart of Antarctica very little snow falls. One reason is that the temperature of the air is too low to contain much water vapor. Another reason is that marine air seldom penetrates deeply into the Antarctic continent. The heart of Antarctica has been compared favorably with the heart of the Sahara Desert in terms of precipitation.

However concerning the pattern of the ice dump, it was not saucer-shaped as it is in Antarctica today, where it is higher toward the periphery where snows fall in greater amounts. Rather the shape was rather conic, some three miles thick at the central nodes, feathering out twenty-five hundred miles in its radius. It may be described as "pancake-shaped," an icy pancake five thousand miles in diameter. Is it possible that ice was suddenly dumped over the magnetic pole some five thousand years ago?

Requirement No. 6
The Flow Pattern of the Ice Mass

The flow pattern of a fluid, suddenly dumped out, is radial, like pancake batter on a griddle, or like milk spilled on the floor. The flow pattern of a fluid, gradually forming and draining over greater lengths of time, is a dendritic or riverlike pattern.

When the ice began to flow, it flowed over hills a thousand feet high, and flowed on for hundreds of miles. It scooped out such basins as Lake Erie, Lake Michigan and the Puget Sound, and, we must suspect, with relative ease. The ice flow did not concentrate in the valleys and avoid the hills. It flowed over both en masse. The radial flow pattern of the Ice Epoch is again suggestive that whatever happened, it happened suddenly.

Requirement No. 7
The Quick-Frozen Mammoths and Rhinos

A vast number of ivory tusks have been gathered throughout Northern Siberia in recent millennia. Demosthenes' father-in-law traded in Siberian ivory. Piano keys of Europe during the seventeenth and eighteenth centuries were made more often from mammoth ivory than from African ivory. One mine in Siberia reportedly yielded twenty thousand tusks. When Vitus Bering, the Danish explorer of the Arctic, visited Bear Island, north of Siberia in the Arctic Ocean, he reported it was composed of two ingredients, mammoth remains and sand. But the predominant ingredient was mammoth bones.

During the eighteenth and nineteenth centuries, reports occasionally came in of mammoths found in a frozen state. Some of these reports were investigated by the Tsarist governments, and a few mammoths were exhumed and brought to St. Petersburg. They were rather sensational evidences of the time when Siberia had had a much more temperate or subtropical climate.

When Baron Toll explored Bennett Island, some three hundred miles north of the Siberian mainland, he reported finding a quick-frozen mammoth, in a land where today, during the height of the Arctic summer, willows will grow perhaps two inches high. This climate is so cold it makes Point Barrow and Alaska look a little like the banana belt. And yet here, Baron Toll found evidence of former life under conditions which today could not possibly exist.

Concerning mammoth bones in Russia, Pallas claimed that there was not a river bed in all Russia, from the Don to the Bering Strait, which did not contain mammoth bones. Other writers have observed that, strangely enough, the farther one goes north, the more numerous are mammoth remains.

Digby, an English explorer of Siberia in the era prior to World War I, listed some twenty-five locations where he knew quick-frozen mammoths and rhinos were found. He reported foliage in a state of partial decomposition yet in their stomachs and mouths, foliage of a temperate to subtropical type.

It should be observed that mammoth remains of the quick-frozen variety occur in the area which was fringe to the magnetic pole, but is rather central to the geographical pole. This is the zone of permafrost in Northern Siberia, but it is also the region which was not glaciated by the Ice Mass due to its greater distance from the magnetic pole.

The mammoths are found, not underfed as if their diet were lichens and willows. Rather they are found, marbled in fat, apparently in the midst of their last delectable dinner, a choice selection of luxuriant herbs. The concentration of blood found in their heads is a strong indicator that they were asphyxiated. To-day, we know that dogs can be out in temperatures around -90° F. for hours and they do not freeze. But these were mammoths, not mere dogs; huge animals clothed in fur.

Sanderson claims that tests have been made, blood-typing these ancient beasts, and in a study of their tissue, a determination of the temperatures surrounding their demise may be ascertained. This is because when an animal dies, water begins to separate within its cells. When it freezes, all separation ceases. The modest amount of water separation in the cells drove Sanderson to the conclusion that temperatures surrounding their demise may have been -150° F. and perhaps lower. This is unearthly cold. What is the explanation? "Out of whose womb came the ice?"

When we viewed the ice on the Antarctic Shelf, and ice in lava formations and ice caves in Eastern Washington, we viewed ice suddenly deposited in a region surrounded by (a) hydrosphere, and (b) magma. If the mammoths were quick-frozen by asphyxiation now we must suspect a sudden eruption of extremely cold atmosphere, on the fringe of the ice dump, perhaps -150° F. or colder.

And beyond that, another correlation must be kept in mind. In much of Europe and North America, quickly-drowned and quickly-buried mammoths and mastodons have been found in many places. Not only must one explain quick-frozen mammoths along with ice caves and ice deposition at oceanic bottoms; one must also bring forth an understanding which accounts for quick-drowned mammoths in some regions and quick-frozen mammoths in others.

This lecturer feels that this synchronism is really not so difficult once one conceives of this entire catastrophic picture involving each of the earth's three fluids in simultaneous upheaval, in tidal activity, and once one views the planet earth caught in a celestial crisis involving simultaneous magnetic and gravitational interaction. This is not difficult. This may be revolutionary in the scientific sense, since it is concerned with revolutionary movements, perturbed orbits, rotations and shifted axes. This does not seem to be very difficult to explain once one gains the catastrophic panoramic picture, but then such basic items should not be very difficult to explain either.

Requirement No. 8
Timing in Terms of the Seasons

The historical timing of this icy catastrophe is one matter, and the seasonal timing is another. Concerning historical timing, for the sake of brevity, we cannot go into reasons why this icy dump is dated around five thousand years ago.

However we shall dwell briefly on its seasonal timing. Frozen sedges, beans, grasses and buttercups in full growth have been found, quick-frozen in Siberia. On many occasions the plants are found bearing seeds, including cones. An elderberry tree was found, quick-frozen with ripe berries in Northern Siberia. Ripe berries suggests that this icy catastrophe may have suddenly come upon that region in the fall of the year. Elsewhere in sedimentary strata, full-grown foliage and fruit impressions similarly are suggestive that their watery demise occurred either in the late summer or in the autumn.

Let us turn briefly back to Genesis 7:11. (Bear in mind that the

Hebrews, prior to the era of the Mosaic Law, counted time from the autumnal equinox, the first day of the year.)

In the second month, the seventeenth day of the month, the same day were all the fountains of the great deep broken up, and the windows of heaven were opened.

The seventeenth day of the second month from the autumnal equinox (Sept. 22) falls around the first week of November. Note by way of coincidence that the quick-frozen vegetation in Siberia appears to have been frozen in its autumnal condition, berries, cones, seeds and all.

Again, may we repeat the oft-repeated question, "Out of whose womb came the ice?" "Speak to the earth and it shall teach thee." "Knowest thou the ordinances of heaven?" Obviously we are just barely skimming the surface of this fantastic, but rather historical subject. Occasionally some scientist may say that it is impossible to quick-freeze a mammoth, or to create ice pockets within lava formations. And yet, there the mammoths are, and there the ice caves are.

Could it be that a scientist, making such quick conclusions, might, at the very least, be considered a rather inadequate historian? Further, is it possible that such a scientist might be making the uniformitarian assumption subconsciously rather than consciously, and thus is never aware of his basic problem interfering with his ability to interpret earth history?

Requirement No. 9
The Location of the Source of the Ice

As previously stated, some fifteen million to twenty million cubic miles of ice was involved. This is 5 per cent to 7 per cent of the volume of the current oceans. It is enough ice which, when melted, might drown the continental shelves about four hundred feet under water, which has happened. For instance, the Hudson Valley does not end at New York Harbor; it proceeds about one hundred miles to the edge of the continental shelf; the last one hundred miles has been drowned in a recent era in earth history. Similar illustrations can be taken from continental shelf locations on other continents.

Where does this much ice exist? How might it be suddenly deposited upon the earth, and over the magnetic regions? As previously mentioned, Saturn's Rings are one example of an icy catastrophe, a fragmentation of an icy celestial wanderer. How much ice is contained in Saturn's Rings? They are ten miles thick, 41,500 miles broad in their band, and 186,000 miles in diameter. Would this be enough ice to form an earth ice epoch?

Callisto, one of Jupiter's larger moons, is considered to be composed mostly of ice, as is Titan, Saturn's largest moon. Many of Saturn's moons have densities indicating they are composed of ices, ices of water, ammonia, cyanogens, hydroxyls and carbon dioxide. Callisto may contain enough ice to make 600 ice epochs the size of the last one which engulfed the earth. In fact a small icy moon, 250 to 280 miles in diameter would contain enough ice for the last ice epoch. In this region of the Jovian planets, Jupiter through Neptune, there is much evidence of vast volumes of ice, and there may be more beyond the Neptune-Pluto realm as far as anyone knows.

If one is looking for ice in vast volumes, ice which might suddenly descend on the earth over the magnetic regions, this is the area for consideration for this is the region where water already well-refrigerated does occur in large volumes.

Concerning the nature of the Ice Epoch, there no doubt will be some questions concerning the mechanics. Figures 2 and 3 are given for assistance in explaining this catastrophic event.

1. The Source. The source of ice was from the remote regions of our solar system, and it was not in evaporated ocean water, a process which requires both gradualness and heat.

2. The Mode of Transport. The mode of transport was by elliptical orbits and across hundreds of millions of miles of celestial space. It was not by planetary wind systems, transporting water vapor, a mechanism which moderates temperatures rather than refrigerates them, a process which melts water more readily than it freezes water.

3. The Method of Deposition. The method of deposition was apparently by collisions of ice particles over the magnetic regions. Such collisions resulted in deceleration, and deceleration resulted in descent.

It would appear that as the earth was engulfed in this gravitational-magnetic catastrophic crisis, either (1) the astral visitor possessed an icy satellite which hit Roche's Limit and fragmentized, or possibly (2) it contained icy rings which were captured (or grabbed) by the earth's superior gravity. The first possibility is the more likely of the two. Roche's Limit for the earth is about ten thousand miles, a location well beyond the ionosphere, and in the magnetosphere.

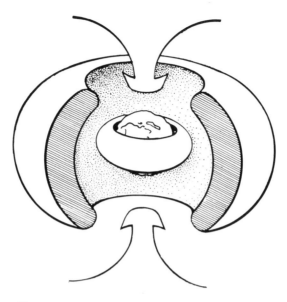

Figure 2 – MANNER OF ICE DESCENT

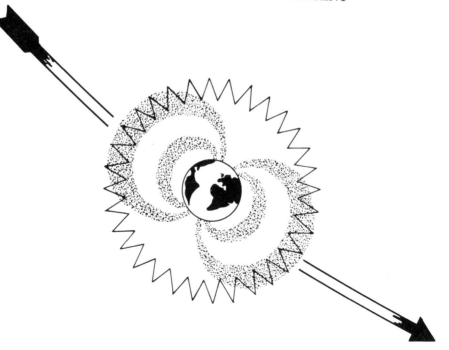

Figure 3 – EARTH'S ORBIT, RADIATION BELTS
& ROCHE'S LIMIT

If such an icy body approached to Roche's Limit, it would fragmentize. The fragments would assume orbits around the earth in response to Kepler's laws, the principles which govern the orbits of man-made satellites.

The strength of the sun's short-wave radiation in the earth's region is very great. And the cold icy particles may be considered as a good dielectric, containing properties, like rubber, of being able to maintain a charge on one side of a particle without dispersing it throughout the particle. Thus, from the short-wave solar energy, an ice particle would pick up a charge.

Relative to rubber, a dielectric, and hair, also a dielectric, one may very easily rearrange the geography of one's hair without even touching it with his comb, providing there are charges of static electricity located on it. Hair will respond to the micro fields and will shift in location.

Similarly, it is suspected, the ice particles which shattered in the earth's magnetosphere, in the range of Roche's Limit, proceeded to pick up a charge from the solar radiation, and the particles were thereby deflected by the magnetic field. Whatever their declination, they orbited around the magnetic poles in patterns something like longitudes, which all merge at the geographic pole.

As these particles shunted around the earth, they tended to collide in the region over the magnetic poles, and in their collisions, they tended to decelerate, and thus descend. Thus we hold that the Ice Epoch was sudden in its approach, magnetic in its pattern, and about five thousand years ago in its timing.

If one begins to view earth history from the catastrophic perspective, quick-drowned mammoths are really not too difficult to explain. Quick-frozen mammoths are also not particularly difficult to explain. Uplifted mountain chains, in great circle patterns, are quite logical if viewed from the perspective of gravitational interaction and internal tides on a rotating sphere.

Obviously, intruding ice particles serve as the perfect nuclei of condensation; hence an antediluvian canopy, the waters above the firmament, just might have been condensed out. They would have had to have been condensed out, setting the stage for a new earth climatology, a climatology based on heat disequilibrium, a climatology featuring deserts, monsoons, tundras, hurricanes, etc. which were unknown in the earlier climatic regime.

It has been concluded that the Ice Epoch may well have been caused by a dump of celestial ice in the magnetic region. Simultaneously, it may well be that some ice came in in lower latitudes, and experienced more friction, and fell in the form of rain, and rain by the buckets.

Thus, while we should look at the Flood crisis in terms of 150 days and nights of gravitational conflict, we should also look at the Ice Epoch phase in terms of something like forty days and forty nights of atmospheric intrusion, and obviously the first forty days and nights, until the reservoir of ice was gone.

Today we occasionally experience sunspots, and resultant magnetic storms, and ethereal auroras in all of their celestial brilliance. The Ice Epoch dump and the auroras have, geographically, an associative relationship. Both are related to the earth's magnetic field.

Thus, in beginning to understand the panorama of catastrophism in earth history, one wonders how the uniformitarian myth could achieve respectability, much less a monopoly in this twentieth century. This certainly must be rated as one of the great jokes of history, the uniformitarian myth in this presumed age of reason. One might reject uniformitarianism, and such associated views as atheism and Darwinism. But one can do much better than this.

We may begin perhaps to peer back to the Flood, and then through the Flood into the antediluvian era. We may begin to understand why it had a finer climatology, a greater longevity, and a more handsome and impressive fauna (animal kingdom).

And beyond this, one may begin to apprehend and appreciate the magnitude of creation, and the majesty of creation. We glean from the Psalms that the stars, those blast furnaces of the galaxy, are merely the fingerwork of God; yet we read that He upholdeth the righteous by the strength of His arms. We note that here, on the earth, on a speck in the universe, one finds this magnificent creation. We note that complexity more than size is miraculous, and what is more complex than man, formed in the image of God?

We are not evolved animals, we are a created race, and though fallen, are nevertheless the finest of a fine creation. For the sake of brevity, rather than consider the majesty of creation further, we may do well to return to the Book of Job. We may view the stricken Job, the righteous, smitten with pain, the objective of Satanic wrath, the heir of eternity, and may we ask, like Job something like this:

Can we "speak to the earth" and anticipate that it will teach us well?

> Out of those womb came the ice; who hath gendered it?
> Knowest thou the ordinances of heaven? Canst thou set the
>   dominion thereof?

Evolutionary Time: A Moral Issue

by R. Clyde McCone

VII

EVOLUTIONARY TIME: A MORAL ISSUE

Introduction

The concept of "evolutionary time" is one that will not be clear to some, and others will take strong opposition to its use. It is necessary, therefore, to introduce this paper with a few words of explanation. What is meant by the term "evolutionary time" is simply the time structure which is an integral part of an evolutionary explanation of man and the universe. This time structure is formed by interlocking, chronologically arranged ages identified by biological, geological, meterological and cultural concepts. The biological sequence of five ages begins some 1½ billion years ago with the Archeozoic (first or primitive life) and is completed with the Cenozoic (recent life). Thus, 1½ billion years of time begins with an age of the lower forms of marine invertebrates and is climaxed by one of mammals, the last of which is man. These biological age concepts are paralleled by geological age concepts beginning with Precambrian. The Cenozoic is paralleled by seven geological ages. The last two of these are the Pliestocene and the Holocene, which cover "roughly" the last million years of time on earth. At least until recently, man's origin was placed at the beginning of the Pliestocene. Therefore, this age was subdivided into three cultural evolutionary stages based on kinds of stone technology and tools, i.e., Lower Paleolithic, Middle Paleolithic, Upper Paleolithic. Glacial periods serve as a parallel system of subdividing the Pliestocene, geological age. The Holocene is post glacial and is organized into cultural stages known as Neolithic, Bronze, and Iron. The Holocene, relatively speaking, is a mere speck of time, being only 25,000 years in duration.

The many attempts to reconcile this system of evolutionary time with the Bible have taken at least two directions. The "gap" theory places an age of chaos of undeterminate length between the first and second verses of the first chapter of Genesis. The six days then become days of re-creation. Another effort has been to regard each of the six days of creation as geological ages which makes room for almost any time system one would choose. Both of these courses take the direction of placing the evolutionary time scale within the process or act of creation itself. The second direction applies the evolutionary time scale to a measurement of the length of time since creation. Hence, we run into such problems as trying to establish whether Adam was Paleolithic or Neolithic man. From the perspective of the creationist the act or process of creation and the length of time since that completed event are two separate problems. This distinction cannot hold for the perspective of the evolutionist since there is one continuous ongoing process that has produced the forms in nature and is in operation today producing the forms of tomorrow.

The first direction of reading temporal-natural processes into the creative act violates Scripture because Genesis presents us with a divine act that brought the whole time-space-matter system of nature into existence. The second direction of using the evolutionary time concepts to measure the time since creation, violates the meaning of which these concepts are integral parts.

I wish to make one more explanatory remark by way of introduction. The approach which will be taken to this topic will be from the position of a believer in Christ and the thought shall be organized within the intellectual framework of cultural anthropology. The Christian is often challenged to defend his position on materialistic grounds, implying that these are the only grounds on which scientific problems can be solved, and that no problems are validly resolved unless they are scientifically resolved. What is often the case is that the problems themselves are outside the sphere of science and the issues are spiritual rather than scientific. I hope to show that such is the case in the problem of the acceptance of "evolutionary time." I have felt free therefore to turn the tables on that so frequently unfruitful conflict of struggling with spiritual issues on materialistic grounds and have chosen rather to deal with the problems of the antiquity of man in the framework of cultural systems of belief and in terms of the moral and spiritual issues which are involved.

Evolutionary Time — A Foundation of Sand for Faith and Morals

There are certain problems very rarely made explicit which both directly and indirectly show that the acceptance of evolutionary time is a sandy foundation for faith and morals. It is a foundation of sand first of all because of a wide gap in knowledge which exists between the professional who presents with authority these ideas and the layman who is expected to be the acceptor of the beliefs. This gap exists, of course, in many areas of our highly specialized culture, but when the issues involved are concerned with the layman's faith, then it is time for some warnings to be issued. One theologian expressed in my hearing the confidence that he without question could accept the authority of the anthropologists in the areas of human antiquity and of human evolution because that is their field. But what if I as an anthropologist should say I will accept the authority of the theologian in regards to the knowledge of God? To which one shall I listen? Some will tell me that God has so predetermined all things that my will or knowledge of Him really makes no difference; others say that God is beyond the reach of human knowledge, and so it is no use trying to know Him; and still others declare to me that He is dead. Anthropologists, too, are not in complete agreement even with regards to evolution or the time involved in it. Where the sandy element for faith and morals comes in is that the layman is expected to accept on the basis of the professional that which he is not in a position to know by any test. Further, the line of communication attempting to bridge the gap to the laymen, itself has many uncertain links. It is usually made up of semi-laymen who write articles for the lay audience, by professionals themselves who attempt to directly influence the lay audience and by the go-between professionals who are professional only in the business of writing text books for elementary and secondary children. An example of the first type is found in an article this past year in the *Long Beach Press Telegram*. Phyllis Battelle wrote an article on the editorial page about Louis Leakey under the title, "Digging Up Man's Origin." In glancing through this article I was somewhat startled when she said that the finds of Leakey were 400,000,000 years old. Leakey claims a mere 1.75 million years age for his finds. So then I read on a little more carefully and found a few sentences later that they had increased to 4 billion years. Perhaps these specific errors of the popular writer are not characteristic. What is more serious is that the popular writer usually speaks with absolute authority while the professional more often structures his statements in terms of the qualifying conditions within which he is thinking and working.

An example of the second type of professional-layman communication is the professional himself writing a semi-popular article for the lay reader. An example of this is the *Life Magazine* publication by Howell. In the introduction the professional physical anthropologist extends his authority as a professional to statements about the Bible and people's beliefs about the Bible — an area in which he is not a professional — in which he is very much in error.

Perhaps the most critical of these attempts to bridge the professional authority-laymen gap in the communication of knowledge is in the writer of textbooks for elementary and secondary schools. Here the layman is a child. The child is not in a position by the use of critical faculties and criteria of judgment to come to a knowledge of what is presented to him. He is expected to receive it by faith in authority. He is confronted with such baseless arguments as, "authorities are agreed," "all intelligent people now believe," etc. He has the additional social pressure of the teacher and his peers. My point is that irrespective of the content truth or untruth of what is being taught, this is not a foundation for faith and morals, nor even for that matter of intelligence. Not even God makes this kind of authoritarian claim on the mind and life of child or adult. He makes the appeal, "Seek and *ye shall find.*" "Taste and *see* that the Lord is good," "Be still and *know* that I am God." The faith of the Bible is not a blind leap into the dark, it is rather a clearly directed step into the light. The result is the knowledge of experience, which is not true for the blind acceptance of authority with respect to evolutionary time.

There is a second and more subtle sense in which the belief in "evolutionary time" proves to be a sandy foundation for faith and morals. That is, "evolutionary time" is not what on the surface it appears to be. Some Bible scholars have been concerned with attempting to reconcile evolutionary-geological-biological-chronology with Biblical chronology by attempting to fit into the evolutionary time scheme the length of time since God created Adam. As the British archeologist, Piggot, has pointed out in his article "Prehistory and Evolutionary Theory" ". . . the past-as-known which is based on archeological evidence is not, and cannot of its nature be, the same as the past-as-known based on evidence which involves the written record in lesser or greater degree" (1960:84). If we follow the position that the Biblical record is also a different frame of reference than that of modern historiography, though nonetheless reliable truth, then the effort to translate or transmigrate Adam across two boundaries from Biblical record to history and then carry history with him into the domain of archeology is not only impossible, it is completely invalid. I have made reference to this idea only to say that the basic problem with evolutionary time, or the antiquity of man, is not to be found in a seeming lack of parallels which it presents to a Biblical chronology correctly or incorrectly perceived. What then is this sub-surface character of "evolutionary time" that is irreconcilable with Christian faith and morals? It is a time system which by its very nature must ultimately deny ultimate origins. The entire scope of this chapter could well be devoted to the clarification and support of this position. Instead, I am only going to give you two or three sentences designed to ferment some thinking within your own mind and leave you to develop your own clarification. In order for any evolutionary system to be complete and consistent it cannot speak of the origin of nature, it cannot speak of the origin of the evolutionary process in nature, and it cannot speak of the origin of time. If from this basic position the evolutionist assumes the origin of life and the origin of man, he has the problem that non-living nature existed eternally without producing life and then it produced life and eventually man. How or why did it get started doing that which it had not done through an eternal existence? The only alternative to this dilemma that I see is that nature has been eternally in the process of creating and destroying life. In either case evolutionary time, great antiquity, or whatever term you choose to use are only deceptive terms for the hidden underlying character which is an eternal time. Some evolutionists are aware of this. Loren Brace of the University of California, Santa Barbara, spoke to an informal gathering of an anthropology faculty and students. One statement made by him is very pertinent here. "Darwin opened up a time scheme that is effectively equal to infinity." It is this that innocent, unsuspecting Christian laymen are not aware of and some Christian scholars appear to be naive about. If what I have said is valid or true, continued research carried on in the framework of evolutionary time will find an increasing antiquity for man. Leakey's work is an example in point.

It is this eternal time that is irreconcilable with Biblical faith. God does not seem to have been as concerned as some people are, or would like Him to be, in establishing the length of time from now to the origin of the world or of man. What is beyond controversy is that, "In the beginning God created the heavens and the earth." There was a beginning, in the beginning was the Word, the Word was God, and He created the universe.

We may conclude then that evolutionary time provides a sandy foundation for faith and morals, first, because of the professional-layman gap which does not lead the layman to what can be called a knowledge of what it claims to teach, and second, because evolutionary time is not what it appears to be. However, evolutionary time has an affect on faith and morals in still another manner because it is itself the basis of a system of values.

Evolutionary Time as the Basis for a System of Values

That person who lives only for the immediate present gratification of his desires with no perspective from the past and no projection into the future is one who is living without a socially provided structure of values. Every social order of man is a moral order in which certain behavior is regarded as good or right and other as bad or wrong and in which the members of the society are motivated according to the common understanding of the past and its focus on their present and in terms of how they see the implications of their present behavior in terms of the future. It is in this sense that every culture has a time structure for values and morals. The significance of a cultural time perspective can perhaps be best seen in the contrast offered by a primitive culture. People with a culture such as the Dakota Indians have a time perspective that is very difficult for Western man to conceive. The meaningful world in which they live is a world without beginning and without end. Miss Deloria, a full-blood Dakota with a Ph.D. in Anthropology, said in a letter to me, "You see we Indians lived in eternity." Furthermore, the past, present, and future are not distinguished and related as they are for Western man. The mythical past has never passed away and is the essence of present reality. This does not make possible the emphasis on a future goal orientation with its important motivation that we know. The Dakota Indian was not striving to get somewhere in this world or the next, he was already there and life was a matter of being, being a Dakota. The Dakota culture was nonetheless a moral order, even though its focus was on the present; it was a present that was significant or meaningful in the manner in which the past and future focused on the present. It was not the valueless life of a sensual present with no concern with past and future. This is the anomic situation of those Indians who have lost the time perspective of their own culture and have not obtained that of Western civilization. I have given this contrasting basis of values of a primitive culture only to more clearly point out that Western man also has a system of values but built on a vastly different time perspective. The early Greek foundation of Western civilization has built into it assumptions about origins, hence we ask questions about origin. The Judeo-Christian tradition, of course, greatly reinforced and concretely defined what among the Greeks was limited to a metaphysical basis for understanding reality. The Christian influence became highly traditionalized in the Middle Ages until there developed a world view and set of values that was built upon a rather specific recent date for the origin of the universe including the world and man. The earth though sinful and imperfect was the center of a universe that was otherwise perceived, since it was the heavens, as being perfect and separated in character as well as space from the earth. The reformation and the renaissance brought liberation to the human mind from the traditionalized restrictions of this world view. It did not, however, develop a system of values that challenged those of the Bible. This direction was taken later when the resources of science were diverted to answer the questions of origins. In 1785, James Hutton wrote in his *Theory of the Earth*:

> For having seen, in the natural history of the earth a succession of worlds we may conclude that there is a system in nature. . . . But if there is a system in nature, it is in vain to look for anything higher in the origin of the earth. The result, therefore of this physical inquiry is, that we find no vestige of a beginning — no prospect of an end (Greene 1961:86).

Hutton did not deny creation or a beginning or an end; it was just scientifically out of sight. Following Hutton, Playfair developed the idea that knowledge of the origin of things was not essential to man; it was enough for him to recognize the handiwork of his Creator in the design of creation. From this he concluded:

> It is but reasonable, therefore, that we should extend to the geologist the same liberty of speculation, which the astronomer and the mathematician are already in possession of; and this may be done, by supposing that the chronology of Moses relates only to the human race (Greene 1961:89).

This strategy of reasoning gained acceptance for belief in the indefinite antiquity of the earth by shunting the objections that would otherwise be raised against it in the name of Scripture.

Subsequent to an increasing degree of acceptance of the antiquity of the earth was the acceptance of the idea of the antiquity of life on the earth. Scriptural objections were silenced by (1) accounting for the appearance of life upon the earth as distinct creative acts of God and by (2) making the appearance of man the final, climaxing and most recent of the Creator's creative acts. As Gruber states:

> On one conclusion . . . all were agreed: The most important of these creations was the last, that in which man appeared, that which Genesis described (Spiro 1965:377).

It remained only for the discovery in Brixham Cave in England, to extend the idea of great antiquity to man. Here in this cave under a stalagmite floor — which would make it of extreme age as understood by Hutton's principles — were found human imple-

ments, stone knives and axes in association with animals long
extinct and believed to be of great antiquity. In the context of the
accepted beliefs this fact constituted evidence that man is, also,
of great antiquity. It was this evidence that converted Charles
Lyell to the acceptance of the antiquity of man. Glyn Daniel in
the *Scientific American* writes that as a result of the discoveries at
Brixham Cave:

> The catastrophist theory was once and for all discarded and with
> it the Biblical notion that the world and man represented unalter-
> able acts of special creation (1959:173).

Later in this same article Daniel concludes that as a result of
Lyell's and others' acceptance of the Brixham Cave evidence:

> The battle was over: the great antiquity of man was an established
> fact. Victorian thought had to adjust itself not only to organic
> evolution but also to the antiquity of man, 4004 B.C. was forgotten
> (1959:174).

Lawrence K. Frank in his book, *Society as the Patient,* shows
how these changing concepts of time are related to moral problems
of modern man.

> Astronomy, geology, paleontology and biology have, during the past
> 300 odd years, given us a totally different time and space per-
> spective in which our earth no longer occupies the central position
> of a recently created universe. The earth has been displaced, rele-
> gated to an insignificant place in the cosmos, but with a past
> history so vast we scarcely can comprehend it, since temporal
> remoteness attentuates our understanding more drastically than
> spatial remoteness. Moreover, man himself has been given a
> radically changed history, in which he no longer appears suddenly
> upon earth by divine creation a few thousand years ago, but slowly
> emerges and evolves from an incredibly long ancestry of mammalian
> prototypes and these in turn from an ever receding horizon of
> living forms. We are today struggling to revise our time per-
> spectives of the past and timidly beginning to explore for the
> inevitable revisions that they involve in our time perspectives of the
> future. Already the focus of personal immortality in an eternal
> heaven has begun to shift and therefore change the dimensions of
> the present. The ascetic conduct that addressed to the immediate
> present, seen as but a proving of our virtue for eternity is beginning
> to lose its coercive appeal. When the present is no longer at-
> tenuated by the focus of eternity, reinforced by the expectation
> of everlasting punishment or bliss, human conduct is bound to
> change. . . . Morals and ethics focused upon the older time
> perspectives lose their authority with every change in the dimen-

sions of time that undermines the cosmic sanctions and necessitates new standards of conduct more consonant with these altered perspectives (1948:354-355).

But Frank realizes that this loss of perspective can lead to the sensual, but utter valueless and meaningless outlook on life expressed in "Let us eat, drink, and be merry." He recognizes that that which he calls the Christian time perspective worked for the people who possessed it; and that we need in our day something like it to take its place, since the time perspective of the antiquity of man has destroyed it. His suggestion goes something like this: Man for the first time in his long evolutionary history has reached the place where because of his knowledge of psychology he is able to change human nature. But this becomes achievable through our children whom we can guide to the future achievement of values. Then in a crucial statement he says:

> Instead of sacrificing the child, as we have from time immemorial, to the values of our other-worldly and superhuman time perspectives, we create a time perspective that expresses the potentiality of childhood as its supreme dimension, to be realized in and through conduct that recognizes the worth of human life, of mating, child bearing and child rearing and the fulfillment of man's physiological and psychological needs (1948:357).

Frank then suggests in place of a belief in the immortality of the human spirit, we substitute a belief in the immortality of the human germ plasm; values are to be biologically and socially based, not spiritually anchored in the supernatural. Here from the pen of one who is a devoted evolutionist is surely a clear and unmistakable testimony to the value structure and its threat to the social values of modern man that is inherent in the evolutionary time perspective.

I believe, however, that Frank does not see beyond a cultural system of values. What he describes is quite an accurate picture of the moral disorganization that characterizes our modern society, and the role that evolutionary time has played in it. As a believer I have to go beyond what Frank is saying and say that the moral character of the followers of Christ is something other than a cultural system of values whatever its time perspective. In place of a time perspective based system of values, a follower of Christ has a Person that is the anchor of his values as is expressed in both the Old and New Testaments. The Psalmist said that "God is *good* to [in the eyes of] Israel even to such as be of clean heart." The Apostle Paul testified that "All things work together for *good*

to those who love God, to those who are the called according to
his purpose." Not only is a changeless and timeless God the focus
of the result of the work of the Holy Spirit rather than a world
view structured in terms of time; "The Holy Spirit also is a witness
to us. . . . This is the covenant that I will make with them after
those days, saith the Lord, I will put my laws into their hearts,
and in their minds I will write them." The moral values of the
Christian are not a social product with its culturally defined time
perspective, but are rather a spiritual product resting on a God
perspective. The point which I wish to emphasize is this: that
while there is a conflict between the values of the evolutionary
time perspective and the traditionalized system based on a time
perspective of some six or ten millennia, the moral disorganization
which Frank observed is chiefly a social phenomenon. Basic issues
for the follower of Christ must necessarily be spiritual issues. I
shall attempt as the final point of this chapter to show that
evolutionary time is itself an ultimate value system that is spiritually
antithetical to and irreconcilable with the ultimate moral values of
the Christian.

The Spiritual Character of Evolutionary Time Values

It may seem rather uncommon to deal with the subject of
evolution in terms of values since it claims in contrast to the
Biblical position to be scientific. The evolutionist claims for his
ideas two of the necessary criteria of natural science, facts and
theory. Some have opposed evolution saying that it is a theory but
has no facts. The position which I wish to present must sound to
many a bit radical. It is that evolution with its time perspective
is neither fact nor theory but is basically a system of values. One
can find a number of expressions among evolutionists that implicitly
betray the fundamental value character of this system. Simpson
(1949:137) protests that some have distorted the evolutionist's
"proper values." A reviewer of Molecules and Evolution (Williams
1967:308) says "Indeed, one might come to the conclusion that the
last genuinely open mind observing and pondering evolution was
Darwin's." However, the thesis that evolutionary time is a value
structure has much more valid support than these kinds of in-
ferences.

It is necessary first of all to make clear what a scientist means
by the terms fact and theory. As Goode and Hatt have pointed out
there is the popular usage of these terms in which theory means
speculation while fact is proven theory. These authors point out
that for the research scientist fact is an empirically verifiable ob-

servation, and theory is the meaningful order or relationship existing between facts. Fact is not to be contrasted to theory as certainty is contrasted to guesswork. Facts are observable events or entities in the world, theory is a system of perceived relationships which constitute an explanation that makes the facts meaningful or understandable to man. Parenthetically I might observe that the Bible lays no claim to being a theoretical explanation of the facts of nature. It is rather a revelation by God of Himself to man. In an article in *Science* George Gaylord Simpson made the claim that evolution was both fact and theory. His position that evolution is fact was supported by his contention that there is consensus or agreement among evolutionists that it had occurred. "No evolutionist has since (Darwin) seriously questioned that man did originate by evolution. . . . No one doubts that man is a member of the order of primates" (1960:969), and so therefore it is a fact. His position that evolution is theory was based on the existence of a large number of differing explanations of how it came about. If evolution were in the strictest sense both fact and theory, it would then be a self explaining fact that would need no explanation — a fact that speaks for itself — which is contrary to the position of science about facts. Perhaps because this claim is made may be the reason why evolution is seldom if ever presented as a theory to be tested or as facts to be explained, but, like values, something to be accepted or rejected.

The position that the ideas of the antiquity of man and of evolution are an integral aspect of a value system rather than scientific theory or empirical fact, is to be understood only in the sense that will be briefly outlined in this chapter. I wish first to point out that for facts to be facts of evolution they have to be facts of transition. Otherwise they are no more than facts of an existing order. It is just such facts that are totally absent. Within the past year a paleontologist commented to me on some of his research that he has been doing in an area in which a continuous sequence of layers of the earth are exposed representing millions of years of geological ages. Then he said, "There is no development of life in any layer in the direction of life above it." His explanation was that on each layer life must have entered from the outside. If there were here examples of transition or development these would be facts of which evolutionary theory would be at least a reasonable explanation. In the absence of these facts the value system generates facts in terms of "what must have taken place."

What is meant then by the statement that evolution is not a theory? One might argue since it has no facts to explain, how can it be a theory? Nevertheless, it does attempt to give explanation to the facts which it generates. In the classification of fossil man in an evolutionary framework from the Australopithicines to Homo Erectus to Homo Sapiens there are assumed to be, though not observed, two great transitional facts in the evolutionary history of man. Allow me to quote from an article entitled "Fossil Man" by Loren C. Eisley:

> Now let me make plain why I chose to remark at the start of this article that man's origin has been greatly clarified but not, paradoxically, the mystery of man. Two facets of that mystery deserve our particular attention:
>
> (1) How did man achieve his upright posture? and,
> (2) How did the human brain arise, and what carried it to its present peak of achievement?
>
> Neither of these questions has in my opinion, been satisfactorily answered (1953:69, 70).

In other words, theoretical explanation of the "generated facts" has never been adequately accomplished. But without evolutionary facts and without evolutionary explanation and with considerable disagreement regarding both the processes and course of human evolution, there is still an unquestioned faith in and commitment to the general idea that it occurred, and that it took "millions" of years to accomplish.

Perhaps the value structure is seen most clearly in the writings of G. G. Simpson who in an article in *Science* magazine speaks of "The world into which Darwin led us." It is also found in his book, *The Meaning of Evolution,* the final chapters of which are devoted to such titles as, "The Search for an Ethic" and "Knowledge and Responsibility." Simpson recognized the need of a new system of values for modern man. He points out that to try to build an ethic on the doctrine of the survival of the fittest simply means that it is good to survive in a tooth and claw struggle for existence. T. H. Huxley concluded from this reasoning that while evolution is a fact, it is ethically bad. But Simpson, after confronting many of the value problems, comes to what he calls the evolutionary ethic. Though evolution in its long process has had no goal and is not purposeful, yet it has produced a creature who does have purposes and goals and who is a morally responsible being. The ethic must then take into account the kind of being which man is, not that from which he has come. Yet it becomes an ethical obligation upon man to make known the truth to his fellow homo sapiens concerning that process which has produced him. How parallel, but irreconcilable, this is to the Christian ethic which says that man is created in the image of God who did have a purpose and that he should glorify his Maker in the knowledge of Him and in making Him known.

According to Simpson the evolutionary ethic is to declare the truth that man has risen, not fallen. It is an ethic that claims not to be absolute but is subject to the new development of cultural, i.e., ethical evolution which makes the process of evolution the absolute in the determination of values. It is an ethic that requires the acceptance of the authority of specialists but the rejection of any absolute authority. It is an ethic which requires "the rejection of revelation or of emotional reaction when knowledge is available." The spiritual challenge which this ethic makes to the faith and morals of the Christian does not need further comment.

We have observed that the values of a Christian find their focus in God — more than that, in a God that is known to the believer — not a God of blind faith. God makes Himself known by expressing Himself, and we have found that the God who at sundry times and in divers manners spoke unto the fathers by the prophets hath in these last days spoken to us by His Son. He it is who hath shed forth His Spirit into our hearts crying Abba Father. I am not here contending that one merely must subscribe to the doctrine of the Trinity. I am stating rather that no God has made himself known to man other than the Triune God of divine revelation. The faith of the Christian is not just believing that there is a God or accepting a God, or the development of a concept of deity. It is rather a mutual faith between a specific person, Jesus Christ, and the believer that produces knowledge based on experience. We often read and sing, "I know in whom I have believed and am persuaded that He is able to keep that which I have committed unto Him against that day." This is the testimony of every believer. It is just such knowledge, faith, and moral values with their focus in the Christ of a Triune God with which evolutionary time as a competing system is irreconcilable.

Earlier in this chapter another trinity was suggested. We pointed out earlier that evolutionary theory inherently could not speak of the origins of nature, the evolutionary process, and time. Hence, it must regard each of these as eternal. These are integral and inseparable units in a trinity of absolute values. Though not explicitly deified as in primitive cultures, a number of characteristics identify nature as the father in the anti-Biblical godhead. In the first place, running through all of the literature, that which for the primitive was Mother Nature is now Father Nature. Nature is the active and sole responsible agent for the production of life and of man. Furthermore, hidden within its mysterious confines resides the unexplainableness of deity. Listen again to Simpson:

> The ultimate mystery is beyond the reach of scientific investigation and probably of the human mind. There is neither need nor excuse for postulation of nonmaterial intervention in the origin of life, the rise of man, or any other part of the long history of the material cosmos. Yet, the origin of that cosmos and the causal principles of its history remain unexplained and inaccessible to science. Here is hidden the First Cause sought by theology and philosophy. The First Cause is not known and I suspect that it never will be known to living man. We may, if we are so inclined, worship it in our own ways, but we certainly do not comprehend it (1949:135).

It seems as though we have constructed here a modern counterpart to that ancient Athenian idol "To the unknown God." The deity of Father Nature is further recognized by Simpson in its changeless authority of the reign of natural law over the processes in it:

> The doctrine of geological uniformitarianism, finally established early in the 19th century widened the recognized reign of natural law. The earth has changed throughout its history under the action of material forces, only, and of the *same* forces as those now visible to us and still acting on it (Simpson 1960:967).

Implicit in this statement is also the changelessness of the forces operating within the framework of the realm of nature bringing about all change and development. The analogy here is clear with the Son as the Word by whom all things were created and through whom all things subsist, and also as "Jesus Christ the same yesterday, today and forever." Evolution as a process in nature in many ways has the relationship parallel to that of the Son to the Father. It is presented as the way — the way all things have come to be, the way that points into the future and even the secret of the way to live and solve our modern problems. Simpson's demonstration of the evolutionary ethic as the foundation for the solution of the problems of modern man makes it no less than a Messiah. It is not only the way, but it is the truth in contrast to which all opposition is referred to as superstition; the worst of it is Evolution is also the life since all life is the product of nature only through the evolutionary process. As we have previously observed, the evolutionary process is without change. The process of evolution is regarded as so absolute and changeless by some that even the ideas about it cannot change. Leslie White protested his being called a neo-evolutionist saying:

Neo-evolutionism is a misleading term: it has been used to imply that the theory of evolution today is somewhat different from the theory of eighty years ago. We reject any such notion (1959:ix).

White goes on to point out that one can no more speak of neo-evolution than of neo-gravitation. And so, one with the Father nature, evolution, the Son who is the way, the truth, and the life, is also without beginning and without change and we may add without end.

The chapter has, however, been focused on time, but a special kind of time, evolutionary time. We have found that it cannot be understood apart from the Trinity of which it is an integral part. It too is without beginning. Time is the spirit of the anti-Biblical Trinity occupying a position opposed to the Holy Spirit of God. It was the Spirit that moved on the face of the waters in the creation account as told in Genesis. At the climax of this sublime disclosure the Triune God said, "Let us make man in our image and after our likeness." It was the breathing of the Spirit into the formed dust of the earth, that one creative act which spanned the line between the non-living and the living and the non-rational and the rational. It is the Spirit, the effective servant, one with the Father and the Son, speaking not of Himself but of the Son and the Father, that is nevertheless the indispensable participant mover in the great act of Creation. But what can be said of the third member of the other trinity that we have called evolutionary time? The parallel role is quite clearly seen in an article by George Wald entitled "The Origin of Life." Here Wald points out two alternatives with which man has confronted the problem of the origin of life: (1) An account of supernatural creation, or (2) a belief in spontaneous generation. He feels that the more rational elements of society prefer to "take a more naturalistic view" which is the latter. But he goes on to point out that modern science through the efforts of Pasteur has discredited the mystical notion of the spontaneous generation of life. He goes further to observe the complexity of life so that the "most complex machine which man has made is but child's play compared to the simplest of living organisms." He goes on still further to show the unbelievable impossibility statistically that the elements of non-living nature could have spontaneously come together to have formed life. But what is his position? "Yet here we are as a result I believe of spontaneous generation" (1954:46). His faith accepts the possibility of the impossible and of the scientifically disproven process. But let Wald give to us the secret of his faith:

The important point is that since the origin of life belongs in the category of the at-least-once phenomena, time is on its side. However improbable we regard this event, or any of the steps which it involves, given enough time it will almost certainly happen at least once. . . .

Time is in fact the hero of the plot. The time with which we have to deal is of the order of two billion years. What we regard as impossible on the basis of human experience is meaningless here. Given so much time, the "impossible" become possible, the possible probable, and the probable virtually certain. One has only to wait: time itself performs the miracles (1954:48).

For the Christian it is the Holy Spirit who is the miracle worker and who establishes the credibility of the entire record in the Word of God. By contrast it is time — evolutionary time — that has wrought the wonders of the universe and makes the evolutionary record of nature credible to the evolutionist. The incongruence of trying to bring them together is seen by the question which would result: How long did it take God to breathe His Spirit into man? Time in no sense can be a factor here. The question how long ago did God create man, whether answerable or not is a question utterly unrelated to the concept of evolutionary time and cannot be approached within its frame of reference.

Conclusion

The spiritual character of evolutionary time leaves the Christian no room for compromise. The follower of Christ needs to be assured that he is the only professional authority with regard to his own experience as a child of God. In this one thing all others are at best, laymen. His experience as a reconciled child of the Father through faith in the sacrifice of His Son Jesus Christ has through the Spirit wrought a miracle in his heart with which evolutionary time cannot compete, nor against which it can make any authoritative challenge. Long ago Joshua challenged Israel with the words: "Choose you this day whom you will serve." Modern man is equally confronted with a moral and spiritual choice that he cannot escape. My choice can be expressed in the words of Joshua, "As for me and my house we will serve the Lord." The inspired author of the majestic, thrilling and wholly credible account of creation had made a similar choice, for it is said of him, "By faith Moses, when he was come to years, refused to be called the son of Pharaoh's daughter, choosing rather to suffer affliction with the people of God . . . esteeming the reproach of Christ greater riches. . . ."

Bibliography

Brace, C. L. and M. F. Ashley Montague
   Man's Evolution. New York: The Macmillan Company, 1965.
Buswell, James O.
   "Adam and Neolithic Man." *Eternity.* Vol. 18, No. 2 (Feb.), 1967, pp. 29-39, 48-50.
Daniel, Glyn
   "The Idea of Man's Antiquity." *Scientific American,* Vol. 201, Number 5 (Nov.), 1959, pp. 167-176.
Eisley, Loren C.
   "Fossil Man." *Scientific American,* Vol. 189, No. 6, (Dec.) 1953, pp. 65-72.
Frank, Lawrence K.
   Society as the Patient. New Brunswick: Rutgers University Press, 1948.
Greene, John C.
   Evolution and Its Impact on Western Thought: The Death of Adam. New York: Mentor Books, 1961.
Piggott, Stuart
   Prehistory and Evolutionary Theory in Sol Tax ed. Evolution After Darwin, Vol. II, *The Evolution of Man,* 1960, pp. 85-97. Chicago: University of Chicago Press.
Simpson, George Gaylord
   The Meaning of Evolution. New York: Mentor Books, 1951.
   "The World Into Which Darwin Led Us." *Science,* Vol. 131, 1960, pp. 966-974.
Spiro, Melforde, E. (ed.)
   Context and Meaning in Cultural Anthropology. New York: The Free Press, 1965.
Wald, George
   "The Origin of Life." *Scientific American* (Aug.) 1954, pp. 45-53.
White, Leslie
   The Evolution of Culture. New York: McGraw-Hill Book Co., Inc., 1959.
Williams, Curtis A.
   "The Ascension and Apotheosis of DNA." *Science,* Vol. 155, 1967, p. 308.

DATE DUE

OCT 27